THE ETYMOLOGY AND USAGE OF ΠΕΙΡΑΡ IN EARLY GREEK POETRY

A Study in the Interrelationship of Metrics, Linguistics and Poetics

ANN L. T. BERGREN
Princeton University

American Classical Studies
Number 2

The American Philological Association
1975

Manufactured in the United States of America by Commercial Printing, Inc., State College, Pa. 16801

Order from Interbook Incorporated
545 Eighth Avenue
New York, N. Y. 10018

Cover drawing by William B. Dinsmoor, Jr.
Studies in the Antiquities of Stobi, vol. II, 1975.

TO

M.A.T.B. and E.F.V.B

To return now to the *Iliad* and the *Odyssey*: it has sometimes been felt that the formulaic, oral style which Homer inherited from the epic tradition could not, since it was not his own creation, have anything to do with his genius, which was to be sought instead in his departures from oral method. But besides the fact that we cannot point to a single certain departure from the method, it must be said that Homer's genius is profoundly involved with the traditional style, and we shall not understand his unique power without first understanding the aesthetics of the style itself. . . . That the formulae are traditional and functional is granted. What else they are remains to be seen.

Cedric H. Whitman

Homer and the Heroic Tradition

CONTENTS

ACKNOWLEDGMENTS viii

EDITIONS x

ABBREVIATIONS xi

INTRODUCTION 1

I. METER, MEANING AND FORMULAIC ART: πεῖραρ in Homeric Poetry 18

A. Formulas with the Plural 21

(1) πείρατα γαίης/Ὠκεανοῖο
One of two concrete meanings of πεῖραρ, the "boundaries" between a land and its opposite element.

(2) πείρατ' ἀέθλων
A metaphor, based upon the concrete meaning and associations of πείρατα γαίης, to be translated, "the boundaries of this world of contests".

(3) πείρατα τέχνης
In this phrase, an appositive of "tools", the concrete meaning of "boundary" is extended to the conceptual notion of "things which define or determine the work of skill".

(4) νίκης πείρατα
Another conceptualization of the concrete function of "boundaries", the "determinants of victory".

(5) ὀλέθρου πείραθ' ἵκηαι
Another metaphorical application of the concrete meaning of πείρατα γαίης, "the boundaries of the land of destruction".

(6) πείρατ' ἀνήφθω/ἀνῆπτον
The second of the two concrete meanings of πεῖραρ, the "bonds" with which Odysseus is bound to the mast.

(7) ὀλέθρου πείρατ' ἐφῆπτο/ἐφῆπται
A metaphor based upon the second concrete sense of πεῖραρ, "the bonds of destruction have been fastened upon" the victim.

B. Fundamental Meaning and Semantic Range of πεῖραρ: "that which forms the limit of the outward extension of anything".

(1) λύοντο δὲ πείρατα πάντα
"All the bonds were loosened."

(2) ἑκάστου πείρατ' ἔειπε
"He explained the determinants of each (event)."

C. Formulas with the Singular

(1) ἄμφω δ' ἱέσθην ἐπὶ ἵστορι πεῖραρ ἑλέσθαι
On the shield of Achilles, plaintiff and defendant go to the judge to get a "determination" of their case.

(2) πεῖραρ ἐπαλλάξαντες ἐπ' ἀμφοτέροισι τάνυσσαν
The concrete meaning, "bond", in a metaphorical description of Zeus and Poseidon encouraging each army equally, so that the Trojans and the Greeks are held in stalemate.

(3) ἐκφυγέειν μέγα πεῖραρ ὀϊζύος ἥ μιν ἱκάνει
A usage that activates all meanings and associations of πεῖραρ: with his step upon Phaiakia, Odysseus will escape the great "bond" and "boundary line" of his misery.

II. THE ETYMOLOGY: πεῖραρ and Rigvedic <u>párvan</u> 62

A. The Meaning of <u>párvan</u> in the Rigveda 65

B. The Meaning of <u>párus</u> in the Rigveda 83

C. The Synonymy of <u>párvan</u> and <u>párus</u> 88

D. The Etymology of <u>párvan/párus</u> and πεῖραρ 94

III. FROM FORMULAIC TO LITERARY ART: πεῖραρ in Archaic Poetry

A. Hesiod -- Describing the Limits of the World 102

Elysium: the Isles of the Blessed
The Hesperides
The πείρατα γαίης καὶ Ταρτάρου καὶ οὐρανοῦ

B. Archilochos -- "Unwinged" Words, Poetic Property and Literary Allusion 115
Fragment 111

C. Alkaios -- Archaism and Modernity: the Duple Character of Lesbian Lyric 119
Fragment Z 27
Fragment Z 21

D. Sixth Century Elegy -- Discovery of Mind and Mannerism: Poetry of Stylistic Transition 132
Solon
Theognis
Pigres

E. Pindar -- Champion of ἁρμονίαι 143
Pythian 4.222
Olympian 2.31
Pythian 1.81-82

CONCLUSION 163

APPENDIX A: R. B. Onians' Analysis of πεῖραρ in Early Greek Poetry 170

APPENDIX B: Metrical Distribution of párvan and párus in the Rigveda 180

END-NOTES 185

BIBLIOGRAPHY 194

INDEX LOCORUM 205

ACKNOWLEDGMENTS

It is a pleasure to record my gratitude to the many who have helped in the making of this monograph. Chiefly, I am indebted to the Editorial Board of the American Philological Association, and in particular, to J. Arthur Hanson, who shepherded the text. To the Committee on Research in the Humanities and Social Sciences of Princeton University and to W. Robert Connor, Chairman of the Department of Classics, I am grateful for research assistance and support in the preparation of the typescript.

This study has been the beneficiary at various stages in its development of generous criticism, correction, insight and encouragement from John H. Finley, Helene P. Foley, Douglas G. Frame, Robert W. Hash, Roger A. Hornsby, Mary R. Lefkowitz, Robert Mondi, Gregory Nagy, Mary L. Philippides, and James N. Rash. Most recently, Richard N. Chrisman and Katherine C. King have lavished upon the text their care and discernment.

Anyone who has made a book can estimate my appreciation of the two who made possible the production of this one. Anne M. Keaney brought both perfectionism and good cheer to the frustrating labor of typing. Thomas N. Habinek contributed unsparingly to every facet of the enterprise his unfailing editorial acumen, his rigorous intelligence, and his excellent taste.

Finally, I extend my deepest thanks to Samuel D. Atkins, who first encouraged the writing of this monograph, who gave me for the work on the Rigveda help beyond what I knew enough to request and, in so doing, a model of teaching and colleagueship.

None of these is responsible for the errors and shortcomings that remain.

Ann Bergren

EDITIONS

Iliad Odyssey Homeric Hymns	T. W. Allen, Homeri opera I-V (Oxford 1917)
Scholia	G. Dindorf and E. Maass, Scholia Graeca in Homeri Iliadem I-VI (Oxford 1874-1888)
Rigveda	T. Aufrecht, Die hymnen des Rigveda (Wiesbaden 1968)
Hesiod	F. Solmsen, Hesiodi Theogonia, Opera et Dies, Scutum (Oxford 1970)
Archilochos Pigres Solon Theognis	M. L. West, Iambi et elegi Graeci I, II (Oxford 1971, 1972)
Alkaios Sappho	E. Lobel and D. Page, Poetarum Lesbiorum fragmenta (Oxford 1955)
Herakleitos	H. Diels, Die Fragmente der Vorsokratiker, 6th ed. rev. W. Kranz, I-III (Berlin 1952)
Pindar	B. Snell, Pindari carmina cum fragmentis (Leipzig 1953)
Scholia	A. B. Drachmann, Scholia vetera in Pindari carmina I-III (Leipzig 1903-1927)

ABBREVIATIONS OF EDITIONS

I - XXIV	Books of the *Iliad*
i - xxiv	Books of the *Odyssey*
LP	E. Lobel and D. Page, Poetarum Lesbiorum fragmenta (Oxford 1955)

All other abbreviations are taken from Liddell-Scott-Jones-McKenzie, *A Greek-English Lexicon*, Ninth Edition.

INTRODUCTION

The work of this century on the metrical and linguistic character of early Greek poetry has been brilliantly productive.[1] The analytical methods developed are highly sophisticated, and the results both subtle and extensive. Despite these technical strides, however, there remain some fundamental problems in the poetics of Epic and Lyric verse.[2] One concerns the artistic merit of the formulaic technique of composition that is typified by the Epics.[3] To many readers a Kunstsprache,[4] a traditional art-language

[1]See Dodds, Palmer and Gray 1968, Holoka 1973 and Griffith 1968 for critical surveys and more bibliography.

[2]Throughout this monograph, the capitalized forms, "Epic" and "Lyric", designate the extant examples of the two genres of Greek poetry, "epic" and "lyric". The term, "Archaic", covers all verse of the seventh and sixth centuries, whether Epic or Lyric. In the historical period Epic poetry is earlier than Lyric. From the pre-historical, i.e., the pre-Homeric point of view, on the other hand, lyric metrical types are more archaic than the epic hexameter, and once both genres are developed, they coexist and alternatively influence one another. On the pre-Homeric interaction between epic and lyric, as well as the historical relations between Epic and Lyric verse, see Nagy 1974, Russo 1974, and Van Sickle 1975.

[3]For an exhaustive appraisal of the work that has shown the Epics to be typical of the formulaic method of verse-making, see A. Parry 1971: ix-lxii. The recent metrical and linguistic studies of Latacz (1968), Ruijgh (1968), Hainsworth (1970), Ingalls (1970, 1972) and Nagy (1974) should be added to those cited by Parry.

[4]For the description of the style by this term, see Witte 1913.

for the extemporaneous composition of verses, is a hindrance to the creative freedom necessary for poetic excellence. The formulaic method of verse-making is also held responsible for those Homeric words of obscure or inconsistent usage that defy our attempts at definition and etymology. These difficulties with Epic style and diction, in turn, mar our interpretation of subsequent poetry. Without a clear comprehension of form and meaning in the Epics, how can we accurately gauge the poetic developments of the Lyric Age? How can we appreciate the transition from "winged words" to literature?

These three problems--the poetic value of formulaic style, the meaning of words in the Epics, and the connections between Homeric and Archaic poetry--persist in part because they have generally not been treated in a manner that mirrors their interdependence. The pursuit of each individually has stopped short of that point where all intersect. Consequently, the modes of linguistic, metrical and poetic analysis developed in recent decades have not been allied in a composite approach to early Greek poetry as a whole.[5] It is just such an approach that is needed, however, for the current status of each of these

[5] For a description of the ways in which metrics, linguistics, and poetics are related, see Jakobson 1960.

three topics indicates that we can best elucidate any one by studying all in concert.

Understanding the technical basis of a work of art should enhance our appreciation of its aesthetic achievement. Or, at least, we should not feel, after learning how a poem is composed, that it is somehow less poetic. Such, however, is the anomalous critical dilemma expressed by many heirs to the Homeric scholarship of the last fifty years.[6] The basic problem is how to describe the aesthetic merits of Homeric poetry without either ignoring or denying the formulaic method, or implying that the poet succeeds in spite of it.[7] The difficulty derives from assuming that this technique of composition, because of its formal strictures, was essentially an inhibition to coherent, creative art and that the genius of the poet or poets of the Epics consists in having overcome it to the extent that they did. This assumption of an inverse rela-

[6]Hainsworth, who in his The Flexibility of the Homeric Formula has made a major contribution toward demonstrating the formulaic nature of Homeric verse, sums up the situation in a recent essay. Hainsworth 1970: 94: "Though it is fairly easy to grasp, with the additional example of Attic drama to assist us, how the use of conventional myth does not impair the force of the poet's vision, it is hardest to understand the art of a traditional diction. To put the matter in its crudest form, can it be art at all that makes use of fixed structures of phrase and sentence, predetermined and almost meaningless epithets, arcane glosses, moribund metaphors and inappropriate similes?"

[7]See End-note A.

tionship between control and creativity, between repetition and originality is so fundamental to our feelings about art and life that we make it easily and often unawares. Yet as long as it underlies our approach to the Epics, not only does our critical dilemma remain unresolved, but it becomes more acute with each new illumination of formal constraint. The premise binds us to definitions of artistic merit that set this style and art at odds.[8]

To remove this critical impasse, we need to reverse our critical assumptions. We must assume that composition through the art-language not merely fails to impede, but in fact provides the means by which poetic excellence in the Epics is created. In order to support this alternate premise, we must show that composing through and not around the force of formal requirements has generated basic units of these poems, namely phrases, that are clearly of high poetic art.[9] Our goal must be to present the formulaic process at work, mediating and motivating

[8]Cf. Stanford 1959: xvii: "And one last warning: the reader must lay aside all contemporary prejudices on the subject of 'originality,' that specious legacy from romanticism, in what follows; otherwise he may easily conclude that Homer's rank as a great poet is being impugned when it is shown how much he owes to his predecessors."

[9]For the criteria defining the "poetic function" of language, see Jakobson 1960.

the expression of the poet's vision.[10]

Directing our effort at a specific example of this process, examining the usage of a single word in terms of formulaic technique, is the best way to proceed. Telescoped attention upon an individual word offers a response to those who admire the Epics' monumental composition,[11] but contend that close reading all too often reveals the building-blocks to be poetically bland.[12] An illustration of the formulaic technique promoting artistic excellence at the level of the word would counter the claim that the

[10]Cf. Whitman 1974: viii: "We will never know what, if anything, is original with Homer himself, but we may learn something of the potentials for development and innovation within a traditional linguistic edifice, and thus perceive some of the factors that govern a poet's use of his medium; one may distinguish the fixed and the fluid elements available for the expression of a given semantic need, and observe how one composer's choice among these affects others. Before this kind of knowledge, the forbidding specter of the rigid formula recedes into the living processes of language at work in the mind, always seeking to clarify and enrich its symbolism; and only with the help of such linguistic understanding can the literary appraisal of a traditional poem be true."

[11]For the view that the originality, and by implication, the poetic virtue of the Epics lies in their overall organization, see Howald 1946 and Greene 1951. Hainsworth 1970: 94 expresses the view of many: ". . . to modern eyes his material is only too obviously traditional. His originality is in the conception of the monumental epic." The studies of Fenik (1968 and 1974) and Segal (1971) show clearly the contribution to this "monumentality" of the artful arrangement and manifold variations of traditional narrative patterns. For an application to Epic of some Structuralist theories of narrative analysis, see Peradotto 1974.

[12]See End-note B.

Epics achieve structural magnificence by means of moribund materials.[13]

The demonstration of formulaic artistry will be most cogent, if the word chosen for examination is one of those presenting inconsistent usage that has confounded attempts at etymology. If one of these words is taken as the object of an effort to portray the aesthetic value of formulaic style, and if this effort resolves the apparently contradictory usages, then the interdependence of form, meaning and poetic merit in the Epics will be all the more clear. If the supposed semantic inconsistencies can be shown to be products of the formulaic method, extending and renewing its resources, then the *Kunstsprache* will emerge as a poetic vehicle like any other, a language in

[13]The attempt to demonstrate a "symbiosis" between the method and the merit of the Epics is directed by Hainsworth toward the level of the word, when he rightly observes (1970: 93): "In general, the more detailed and specific the criticism, the more relevant is the theory of oral composition." Cf. also Whitman 1974: ix: "A single formula may seem like a small key with which to unlock so vast a storehouse of tradition, but the role of analogy is a large one in the world of oral creativity, and what is observable of one formula is *mutatis mutandis*, compatible with the development and behavior of others. It would require an intolerable length of pages to describe the full activity of all the component elements of an oral system, but fortunately it is not necessary. Knowledge is qualitative, not quantitative, in that one rightly observed process reveals the dynamics that control all kindred processes, and so brings ultimate principles within reach."

which poets create not by opposing but by manipulating, not by violating but by fulfilling the forms it provides. Moreover, the results of current attempts to define Homeric words suggest that Epic usage must be examined in terms of the technical characteristics of formulaic style, even if the goal is the determination of meaning alone.

The noun πεῖραρ is one of those words which have posed problems of definition and resisted etymology. Why compilers of Homeric lexicons have found difficulty in glossing this and other Epic words is suggested by Émile Benveniste in a recent study which also offers a method for resolving semantic perplexities. In his _Vocabulaire des Institutions Indo-Européennes_, he observes:

> It must be said, however, that our knowledge of Homeric vocabulary is still in its infancy. We have received from antiquity a system of interpretation to which we continue to adhere and which marks our lexicons and our translations. Although a considerable effort has been expended to restore a reliable text and to define the dialectical characteristics of the epic language, our interpretations remain largely those of an age in which aesthetic conventions took precedence over concern for exactitude. The more one studies the Homeric texts, the more one perceives the distance between the real nature of these concepts and the image of them given by the scholarly tradition.[14]

Benveniste's alternative method for determining the meaning of Homeric words is two-fold: (1) abandoning the glosses assigned by dictionaries and commentaries, he forms a defi-

[14]Benveniste 1969: II.58. The translation is mine.

nition solely from contextual analysis of each usage,[15] and (2) the meaning thus derived is compared with earlier Indo-European cognates, whenever such exist. The comparison makes it possible to "work forward," from the historical point of view, upon the Homeric texts, i.e., to look at a word from a more ancient period to see if it sheds light upon the meaning of a word in the Epics.

The hazards in either omitting contextual analysis or "working backward" to solve semantic problems are illustrated by previous attempts to define πεῖραρ. The question is whether or not πεῖραρ is homonymic, for in some cases it seems to mean "end, boundary" and in others, "a tied rope". Many scholars assume that the word is a homonym.[16] Others have tried to account for these two denotations by claiming that one is derived from the other. To support his view that Latin _ora_ means "borderline" and is related to _ora_, designating "a rope to bind ships to the shore",

[15] Benveniste 1969: II.59. On this effort to determine a basic signification common to every usage, see also Thieme 1957: 54-55.

[16] Supporters of πεῖραρ as a homonym include: Doederlein 1863: on XIII 358-360, Merry and Riddell 1886: on xii 51, and Schulze 1892: 109f., 166f. Krause (1936: 148f.) observes that no systematic investigation underlies Schulze's opinion. Krause's own theory, however, is similar and according to Frisk (1960-1970: s.v. πεῖραρ) unsound. Krause proposes that the root of πεῖραρ = "ende, grenze" is *per = "over, across, through", while that of πεῖραρ = "Seile" is an asigmatic form of *sper = "turn, rotate, revolve, twist".

Niedermann cites πεῖραρ as an example of a word for "rope" that also means "boundary".[17] He accounts for the development from "rope" to "boundary" by asserting that from oldest times, cables or cords were used at the division of estates for the measurement and thus for the demarcation of individual parts. The scope of Niedermann's study, however, does not entail any efforts to demonstrate his interpretation with evidence from Greek texts. He assumes that πεῖραρ = "rope" and πεῖραρ = "end, boundary" are not homonymic, and interpolates an explanation for the two meanings based upon a second assumption, i.e., that the first meaning is primary. Furthermore, Niedermann leaves out of account the usages of the word for which neither of these two glosses appears adequate.

Only G. Björck has attempted a comprehensive account of all the early usages of πεῖραρ.[18] Björck believes that

17Niedermann 1931: 7f.

18Björck 1936-1937: 143f. Onians 1951 devotes a chapter (pp. 310-342) to the instances of πεῖραρ in the Epics and the poetry of Archilochos and Pindar. Because his discussion aims at a comprehensive explanation of the early usage of the word, it provides a useful measure of the methods of analysis and the conclusions offered in this monograph. Accordingly, Onians' account will be examined in Appendix A in terms of the three-part procedure for determining meaning advocated here and in light of the results it yields. It has not been possible to take account in this monograph of the discussion of πεῖραρ in Detienne and Vernant 1974. To do justice to its merits and failings would require nothing less than an appendix like that devoted to Onians' analysis.

bout ("end"), in both the concrete and the figurative sense, is the primary meaning of the word. He objects to the theory of Niedermann on the grounds that πεῖραρ never designates the line of demarcation between two similar domains, but always the extreme limit of any element. On the assumption that πεῖραρ means bout, Björck attempts to demonstrate that all Homeric usages of the word derive from this primary signification. His method is to work backwards, from the chronological point of view, by using Classical and post-Classical instances of πεῖραρ to explain those in Homeric and Archaic poetry.

Björck's study exemplifies the limitations of defining the early by the late. Subsequent usages of πεῖραρ provide glosses that are consistent with some but not all of the Homeric occurrences. For example, Björck candidly despairs of explaining πεῖραρ in

πεῖραρ, ἐπαλλάξαντες, ἐπ' ἀμφοτέροισι τάνυσσαν.

XIII 359

He maintains that every other context where πεῖραρ seems to mean "rope" is merely a special case of the concrete sense of bout. In those cases, πεῖραρ means the "end" of something, namely a rope. Of this line, however, he says only, ". . . and the gods hold at the same time some kind of celestial rope; that is, to tell the truth, a concept difficult to accept and incompatible in any case with the concrete style of Homer."[19] This usage of πεῖραρ demands more attention, if we are to account for the total semantic range of the word. It is the only time in Epic or Lyric when πεῖραρ is described in any greater detail than μέγα (ν 289), τὰ νείατα (VIII 478) or πάντα (*h*. *Ap*. 129). The complete sentence is:

> τοὶ δ' ἔριδος κρατερῆς καὶ ὁμοιΐου πτολέμοιο
> πεῖραρ, ἐπαλλάξαντες, ἐπ' ἀμφοτέροισι τάνυσσαν
> ἄρρηκτόν τ' ἄλυτόν τε, τὸ πολλῶν γούνατ' ἔλυσεν.
>
> XIII 358-360

If a definition derived from Classical idioms is at odds with such an elaborate instance of the word, it is appropriate to try the approach of Benveniste.[20]

To Benveniste's two-part method of explicating Homeric words, a third procedure must be added. Besides being free from pre-conceived glosses provided by Classical usage, the examination of contexts must also include an attempt to determine the part played in each usage by the technical characteristics of Homeric style. Benveniste's own analysis of κῦδος exemplifies the inadequacy of a definition formed without regard to the

[19] Björck 1936-1937: 146-147.

[20] The additional instances in which Björck's interpretation seems insufficient will be discussed in notes to the examination of individual contexts.

formulaic character of Epic diction. On the basis of the appearances of κῦδος, especially those of *Iliad* V, where Athena bestows it upon Diomedes, Benveniste concludes:

> Here is the fundamental character of *kûdos*: it acts as a *talisman of supremacy*. We say a *talisman* because the giving of *kûdos* by a god procures an instantaneous and irresistible advantage, in the manner of a magic power, and the god accords it now to one, now to another, according to his will, and always in order to give the advantage at the decisive moment of a combat or a rivalry.[21]

This explanation of κῦδος conforms with several Homeric contexts of the word, and when discussing those lines, Benveniste is convincing. His argument begins to seem strained, however, when he turns to other collocations (e.g. κῦδος ἀρέσθαι) where the word seems to mean "glory". About these examples he is forced to admit that

> . . . *kûdos*, which is properly the talisman of triumph, has slipped from the sense of "triumph" in the expression "to carry away kudos," by a transition that one can imagine: the hero, having accomplished an outstanding exploit, carries away by his valor that *kûdos* which only a god can accord; in a way he plunders it from the god. Thus the formula, *kûdos arésthai*, enters into the repertory of heroic praise, under the same title as *kléos arésthai*, "to carry away glory" (Il. 5,3).[22]

Yet he earlier claimed that

> In epic terminology, we must be convinced of this, the major terms are all specific and know no synonymy. A priori, *kléos*, "glory", and *kûdos* are not equivalents, and, in fact, as we shall see, *kûdos* never signifies

[21]Benveniste 1969: II.60.
[22]Benveniste 1969: II.65-66.

"glory".[23]

The inconsistencies in Benveniste's argument raise questions of fundamental importance to the definition of Homeric words and the appreciation of formulaic style. Must all instances of a given word in the Epics necessarily reflect the same stage of semantic development? Under what conditions and to what extent do the internal dynamics of the formulaic technique affect the usage of words? For example, did the desire for a formula like κλέος ἀρέσθαι, but with a trochaic (κῦδος = - ᴗ vs. κλέος = ᴗ ᴗ) opening, motivate the collocation of κῦδος ἀρέσθαι with some accompanying generalization of the semantic force of κῦδος?[24] Questions such as these make it clear that any interpretation of any word in the Epics must consider the ways in which the formulaic form of the poetry might affect meaning.

The demonstration of formulaic artistry and the determination of meaning in the Epics are thus interrelated goals. The pursuit of each leads to the need for a common method of investigation, combining metrical, linguistic and poetic analysis. The contexts of a word must be examined, with no current glosses in mind. At each

[23]Benveniste 1969: II.59.

[24]On the semantic similarities between κῦδος and κλέος see Schmitt 1967: 78-79, 87-89.

occurrence our aim must be to explain what the word means and how its poetic effects were created, not despite but by means of the formulaic method. The basic sense emerging from the Homeric usages must then be compared with Indo-European cognates. On the basis of this comparison an etymology can be attempted. The results of these procedures, in turn, provide a basis for treating the third of the critical problems described at the outset, the relations between Epic and Lyric poetry.

In two ways, one more widely recognized than the other, Homeric and Archaic poetry cast light on each other and must be studied together. Insofar as Epic precedes and influences the poetry of the seventh and sixth centuries, we cannot comprehend the poetic achievements of this period without reliable understanding of the style and meanings of the _Iliad_ and the _Odyssey_. And, conversely, we set in sharper focus the art-language represented by the Epics, by discerning the stylistic developments subsequent to the introduction of writing. In order to see in a systematic way how poets from Hesiod to Pindar repeated, refashioned or departed from the forms and meanings inherited from Homeric diction, we need to compare the Epic usage of a word with its occurrences in Lyric verse.

By examining a word in both Homeric and Archaic poetry

we also gain an opportunity to test some recent qualifications of the assumption that all dialectical forms shared by Epic and Lyric constitute imitations of or allusions to the earlier by the later verse. For example, the occurrence in a fragment of Alkaios of the genitive plural of πεῖραρ, πειράτων, is described as "epic imitation" by the definitive grammar of the language of Sappho and Alkaios, because the form exemplifies the 8th century Ionic and not the contemporary Lesbian treatment of digamma.[25] This automatic inference of artificial Epic usage may not, however, be justified. The recent work by Gregory Nagy on the connections between the meter and language of Epic and Lyric suggests that the relations between the two are more complicated than we have supposed.

Nagy starts from the long recognized fact that the metrical types in extant Lyric are, by virtue of their characteristic lengths of fixed numbers of syllables, Indo-European in origin. They are older in form than the hexameter of extant Epic, which shows the relatively later, Greek innovation of admitting a long syllable for two short syllables.[26] With the evidence provided by the usage of the phrase κλέος ἄφθιτον in Epic and Lyric and of

[25]Cf. Hamm 1958: 18, 41. See Chapter III, n. 18.
[26]Nagy 1974: 27-149.

the Sanskrit cognate _śrávas ákṣitam_ in the Rigveda, Nagy proposes (1) that the hexameter of Epic is derived from an isosyllabic metrical form that happens to be preserved in the lyric meter of the chronologically later Sappho 44, (2) that as the hexameter was fashioned from a lyric meter, so the phraseology of the pre-Homeric epic lines was made up of formulas used in that lyric verse-type, and (3) that there was a separate, parallel inheritance by Lyric poets of formulaic material cognate with that received by the Epic poets. Nagy's conclusions, if true, are important beyond the immediate sphere of metrics and linguistics. They are crucial to the literary criticism of Archaic poetry. They imply that Lyric poetry is not necessarily a chronological and derivational monolith. Some poems may seem to show Epic imitation, while in fact displaying traditional lyric diction, independently inherited. Some verses may be modern in the ways customarily assumed; others may exemplify language of extreme antiquity.

One of these archaisms may be Alkaios' usage of πειράτων, for its scansion, - ᴗ -, is not only that of the 8th century Ionic form of the word, but that of its original, Indo-European form, as well. In order to determine the status of this occurrence of πεῖραρ, we must see whether it accords with what Nagy's theories would predict about the relations between the Lyric usage and the instances of πεῖραρ in the Epics. Here, we encounter a problem in the generic relations of early Greek poetry, requiring a metrical, linguistic and poetic analysis of Lyric that, in turn, depends upon the application of a similarly integrated procedure to the Epics.

The fitness of the noun, πεῖραρ, for a paradigm of this method of study, consists in its being a Homeric word of disputed meaning, with a morphological cognate in Rigvedic Sanskrit, *párvan*, and an extensive, problematic and poetically important usage in Archaic poetry. To illustrate the relation between meter, meaning and poetic excellence at the level of the phrase, each Homeric instance of πεῖραρ will be examined in Chapter I. Chapter II will compare the fundamental meaning of the word in the Epics with the Rigvedic occurrences of *párvan*. The aim will be to determine whether πεῖραρ and *párvan* are semantically as well as morphologically cognate. On the basis of the Homeric and Rigvedic meanings of the word, an etymology will be proposed for an original Indo-European, **per-u̯s/ u̯ṛ/ṇ*. After the etymological and the stylistic background of πεῖραρ has been established, Chapter III will treat the occurrences of the word in the verse of Hesiod, Archilochos, Alkaios, Sixth Century Elegy and Pindar with the same combination of metrical, linguistic and poetic analysis that was applied to Homeric poetry. We will concentrate our attention on the ways in which the cavalcade of usages of πεῖραρ in Archaic poetry presents in microcosm the stylistic developments of the period as a whole.

I. METER, MEANING AND FORMULAIC ART: πεῖραρ in Homeric Poetry

The prospects for revealing formulaic artistry and resolving the semantic difficulties with πεῖραρ are at first quite dim. Of the singular forms in Epic, each is obscure both in meaning and in meter. No translation is certain, and the various glosses suggested by the contexts seem to have no semantic ties. Each usage occupies a different position in the line. This metrical variation is in itself, however, relatively unimportant, for the singular, πεῖραρ, occurs only three times, too few to certify any particular metrical characteristics for the word, even if all three instances occupied the same place. As far as meter is concerned, the twenty-two occurrences of the plural, πείρατα, offer a better view of poetic practice.

Unlike the singular, the plural of πεῖραρ displays strict metrical regularity in hexameter poetry: it opens an Adonic segment. The unelided πείρατα, - υ υ, combines with a word shaped - ⏓, or the elided πείρατ'/πείραθ' joins a word shaped υ - ⏓, to form a unit of the shape, - υ υ - ⏓, often called Adonic after the Sapphic refrain, ὦ τὸν Ἄδωνιν (168 LP). As J. B. Hainsworth has demonstrated, these Adonic formulas occur most frequently at the following two positions in the hexameter line:[1]

– ∪ ∪ – ∪ ∪ – ∪ ∪ – ∪ ∪ – ∪ ∪ – ∪

Adonic formulas may be interchanged between these two slots, provided the final syllable is short. Of the twenty-two instances in Homeric poetry of the plural forms of πεῖραρ, twenty, following the bucolic diaeresis, open line-final segments, and two, falling in the second foot, begin mid-verse Adonic formulas. The two mid-verse phrases are made up of the elided form, πείρατ'/πείραθ', and a verb, of which the final vowel is short either by nature or by correption. Homeric diction employs the plural of πεῖραρ only within these technical limitations.

In contrast with the uniform metrical character of all instances of πείρατα, the meanings of the word have appeared to be so contradictory that attempts to reconcile them all have ended in the declaration of a homonym. The following two lines display the semantic poles that have presented the problem:

οὐδ' ἔτι δεσμά σ' ἔρυκε, λύοντο δὲ πείρατα πάντα.

h. Ap. 129

ἕζετ', ἐπεὶ ᾧ παιδὶ ἑκάστου πείρατ' ἔειπε.

XXIII 350

[1]Hainsworth 1968: 48-53, and tables, 136-138. See also Nagy 1974: 61ff.

In the first verse, πείρατα appears to mean "knots" or "ropes", while "end" or "fulfillment" seems to be the sense of the second usage. Even this degree of semantic divergence, however, is accounted for when the remaining instances of πείρατα in Epic are surveyed in the manner outlined in the Introduction.

At each occurrence of the word two questions are asked. If this context alone is examined, what meaning emerges for πεῖραρ? What is the relationship between the formal characteristics of this usage and the poetic force it carries? The combined results of this contextual analysis begin to resolve the difficulties with the meaning of πεῖραρ, for they reveal that each usage was created by manipulating and extending, within the regular operations or "grammar" of the art-language, a fundamental sense that spans the semantic range of the word. At the same time, the poetic properties of each instance are seen to result from fulfilling, and not from circumventing, the formal exigencies of the style.

In light of the basic sense of πεῖραρ derived from the usage of the plural, the instances of the singular do not appear so semantically arcane. Indeed it is in the following lines, where the meaning of πεῖραρ has seemed most obscure, that the poetic potential of the word is shown to be most fully realized.

τοὶ δ' ἔριδος κρατερῆς καὶ ὁμοιΐου πτολέμοιο
πεῖραρ, ἐπαλλάξαντες, ἐπ' ἀμφοτέροισι τάνυσσαν,
ἄρρηκτόν τ' ἄλυτόν τε, τὸ πολλῶν γούνατ' ἔλυσεν.

XIII 358-360

καὶ δὴ Φαιήκων γαίης σχεδόν, ἔνθα οἱ αἶσα
ἐκφυγέειν μέγα πεῖραρ ὀϊζύος, ἥ μιν ἱκάνει·
ἀλλ' ἔτι μέν μίν φημι ἄδην ἐλάαν κακότητος.

v 288-290

Although the rarity of the singular still precludes specification of its metrical characteristics, it is nevertheless clear from analysis of the Epic usage of the other words in these passages that the formulaic method of verse-making motivated each expression. Most of the other words occur often enough in Epic to warrant a generalization of their formulaic properties, and those properties are found to be illustrated in these particular instances with πεῖραρ.

A. Formulas with the Plural

(1) πείρατα γαίης/'Ωκεανοῖο

Five times in Homeric poetry the plural of πεῖραρ clearly denotes the ends of the earth. The sense is concrete. The πείρατα γαίης are the physical extremities of the earth. When you stand upon the land by the farthest sea, when with one step forward you will leave the land behind, you stand upon the πείρατα γαίης. It is a precarious position. It is the line between opposite elements, the limit of the human world. Once the phrase describes a nearer shoreline, one within this world.

In ix 283ff. Odysseus craftily circumvents Polyphemos' attempt to determine the location of his visitor's ships. Odysseus claims that:

νέα μέν μοι κατέαξε Ποσειδάων ἐνοσίχθων,
πρὸς πέτρῃσι βαλὼν ὑμῆς ἐπὶ πείρασι γαίης,
ἄκρῃ προσπελάσας·

The picture here is particularly clear. Sheer against the sea is a rocky promontory. Odysseus' ship is dashed against its face, the πείρατα of the Cyclops' land. The πείρατα are, in this case, the πέτραι, because it is the rocks which form the boundary between the island and the sea. It might seem that πείρατα here means the "end points" of the shore, the jutting cliffs and the breakwaters, but the remaining examples of this formula, the πείρατα γαίης/ 'Ωκεανοῖο, argue against this interpretation. Together they also suggest that formal as well as semantic considerations underlie the choice of πείρατα here, and invite a reconsideration of the rhetorical subtlety that those accustomed to the Epic art-language might have perceived in Odysseus' use of the formula.

That πείρατα means lines of demarcation and not a series

of discrete end-points is proven by the uses of the word to describe the ultimate meeting of land and sea. At the circumference of the earth lies not only the πείρατα γαίης but also the πείρατα Ὠκεανοῖο. The Hymn to Aphrodite provides the composite picture. During his blooming youth, Tithonos

Ἠοῖ τερπόμενος χρυσοθρόνῳ ἠριγενείῃ
ναῖε παρ' Ὠκεανοῖο ῥοῇς ἐπὶ πείρατα γαίης·

226-227

All along the shoreline of the earth the streams of Ocean flow. And all along the streams of Ocean lie the πείρατα γαίης. Thus Hera, in her specious request for Aphrodite's girdle, says:

εἶμι γὰρ ὀψομένη πολυφόρβου πείρατα γαίης,
Ὠκεανόν τε, θεῶν γένεσιν, καὶ μητέρα Τηθύν.

XIV 200-201=XIV 301-302

The πείρατα γαίης, therefore, are of the same shape as the Ὠκεανός. "The sea is the land's edge also."[2]

When you stand in the streams of Ocean, when your next step will fall upon the land, you stand upon the πείρατα Ὠκεανοῖο. And you might be standing in front of the city of the Kimmerians, located παρὰ ῥόον Ὠκεανοῖο, in eternal, sunless night. There Odysseus sailed to reach the entrance

[2]T. S. Eliot, Four Quartets, "The Dry Salvages", I.

to Hades:

῾Η δ᾽ ἐς πείραθ᾽ ἵκανε βαθυρρόου ᾽Ωκεανοῖο.
ἔνθα δὲ Κιμμερίων ἀνδρῶν δῆμός τε πόλις τε.
xi 13-14

This conjunction of the elided πείραθ᾽ with the verb ἵκανε illustrates the use before the trochaic caesura of Adonic formulas with a short final syllable. The phrase here is cognate with such line-final usages as

οὐδ᾽ εἴ κε τὰ νείατα πείραθ᾽ ἵκηαι
γαίης καὶ πόντοιο, ἵν᾽ ᾽Ιάπετός τε Κρόνος τε
ἥμενοι οὔτ᾽ αὐγῇς ῾Υπερίονος ᾽Ηελίοιο
τέρποντ᾽ οὔτ᾽ ἀνέμοισι, βαθὺς δέ τε Τάρταρος ἀμφίς·
VIII 478-481

The specification provided by the genitive in the line-final πείρατα γαίης phrase is here achieved by enjambment: γαίης is placed first in the following line. A semantic variant for ᾽Ωκεανοῖο is found in καὶ πόντοιο, filling the second line up to its central juncture.[3]

Not only Hades but also Elysium lies at the πείρατα γαίης. In the earliest description of the abode of the blessed, Proteus prophesies Menelaos' future bliss:

ἀλλά σ᾽ ἐς ᾽Ηλύσιον πεδίον καὶ πείρατα γαίης

[3]For more myths and poetic motifs associated with the πείρατα ᾽Ωκεανοῖο, see Nagy 1973.

ἀθάνατοι πέμπουσιν.

iv 563-564

Here the force of the orthodox position of the formula at the end of the verse motivates an emphatic hysteron-proteron. The resulting reversal of the actual order of arrival, in the manner of a hyperbaton, focuses attention upon the πείρατα γαίης and thus upon the extreme remoteness of Elysium.

Taken together, these contexts of πείρατα γαίης/ Ὠκεανοῖο paint a precise picture of the meaning of πείρατα. The edge of a land, the πείρατα γαίης, could be conceived of as jagged, a series of end-points, but the border of the sea, the πείρατα Ὠκεανοῖο, could not. If πείρατα denotes the extremities of each region, it must surely mean continuous lines, whether zig-zags, defining the crags of Polyphemos' island, or the circle around the world. The plural appears to serve a technical as well as a semantic purpose in these formulas. Its dactylic shape facilitates the formation of an Adonic segment, which is itself helpful, because of its interchangeability between line-end and mid-verse positions, in composing whole hexameter lines. Semantically, at any rate, πείρατα in these formulas denotes the lines that define land and sea, earth and Ocean, and the world of the living and that of the dead in Hades or Elysium.

In view of the frequency of the use of πείρατα γαίης as "the perimeter of the world", it seems that Odysseus' use of the formula lends his lie to Polyphemos an irony that was not at first apparent, an irony that is typical of the hero and emblematic of the artistry of the diction that created him. Odysseus refers to Polyphemos' island by means of the formula that is the "word" in Epic diction for the limit of the human world, i.e., πείρατα γαίης at the end of the verse. By recalling this frequent meaning of the formula, Odysseus' usage would invite someone steeped in Epic poetry to compare the two boundary lines. Here, as elsewhere, then, Odysseus' falsehood is ironic because of its foundation in fact. The πείρατα of Polyphemos' island are analogous to the ultimate border of the earth. Once crossed, the boundary of Polyphemos' island almost becomes the threshold of Hades for Odysseus, as the monster's cave almost becomes the hero's tomb. The Cyclopes have counterparts in Giants like Iapetos and Kronos.[4] Their world is like Elysium in its innocent, idyllic, spontaneous fertility.[5] In their ignorance of Zeus and the cultural structures of family, assembly and guest-

[4]Cf. VIII 479, p. 25.

[5]Cf. iv 563, p. 26. On the extraordinary fertility of Elysium see Hesiod _Op_. 166-174: there the earth puts forth an abundant harvest three times a year. Cf. also Pindar, _O_. 2.68-77.

friendship, the Cyclopes live in a manner militantly antithetical to civilized human existence. Their island has the characteristics of the other side of the world, but Odysseus is one of the heroes who does reach the ultimate πείρατα γαίης, cross them, and return to tell the tale, as he is telling it now at Alkinoos' palace.[6] His use of the πείρατα γαίης formula would recall this fact, and in turn, forecast his escape from Polyphemos.

(2) πειρατ᾽ ἀέθλων

Just as the allusive force in the concrete sense of πείρατα γαίης is activated by Odysseus' response to Polyphemos, so the potential in this formula for metaphor is realized by the choice and arrangement of his words at xxiii 248. At the end of the conversation in which Odysseus relates to Penelope the many trials he endured in order to reach home, the hero sighs:

ὦ γύναι, οὐ γάρ πω πάντων ἐπὶ πείρατ᾽ ἀέθλων
ἤλθομεν, ἀλλ᾽ ἔτ᾽ ὄπισθεν ἀμέτρητος πόνος ἔσται.

The use of πάντων and ἐπὶ seems to be a composite of patterns in the πείρατα γαίης formulas. In πολυφόρβου

[6]Heracles is another hero who returned from the πείρατα γαίης; see Hesiod, Th. 517-532: Heracles encounters Atlas πείρασιν ἐν γαίης. On this instance of the formula, see p. 112. For an overt correlation of the analogous activities of these two heroes by means of the manipulation of formulaic diction, see n. 41 on v 288-290.

πείρατα γαίης (XIV 200-201) we see the order, adjective-in-genitive + noun + noun-in-genitive, evident in πάντων . . . πείρατ' ἀέθλων. With the addition of ἐπὶ the phrase becomes analogous with ἐπὶ πείρατα γαίης (h. Ven. 227), and particularly with ὑμῆς ἐπὶ πείρατα γαίης (ix 284), which shows the full adjective-in-genitive + ἐπι + noun + noun-in-genitive word order.

If πάντων ἐπὶ πείρατ' ἀέθλων was composed on these sorts of models in order to make figurative use of the concrete meaning of πείρατα in πείρατα γαίης, Odysseus is saying that he has not yet reached the ultimate boundary line of his "world" of contests, the πείρατα (γαίης) ἀέθλων. Another tract still awaits him, the journey inland to the people who have never seen the sea. There, in planting the oar, he will perform his final propitiation of Poseidon. The implication of the metaphor is that only this reconciliation with Poseidon will permit Odysseus to enter a "world" of peace, which differs from the life of struggles set by the god (within the πείρατ' ἀέθλων) as the region of Ocean, Hades and Elysium differs from the world of mortal life (within the πείρατα γαίης). The metaphor, therefore, indicates that the hero understood well the prophecy of Tieresias, for it is after Odysseus has reached this πείρατ' ἀέθλων, the planting of the oar, that he will, as the prophet said, arrive at the limit of his human life, his peaceful passing beyond the πείρατα γαίης into death.[7]

Some scholars have taken πείρατ᾽ ἀέθλων to be a metaphor but of a different sort and not related to the meaning of πείρατα γαίης. Krause mentions the opinion that πείρατα here means τέλος or "Zeitseil", but acknowledges that the institution of a "goal-rope" cannot be proven.[8] To other readers, πείρατα indicates merely "the end", with no specific connotations. Such readers might object to the interpretation offered above on the grounds that in Epic, characters generally do not express themselves metaphorically, and that an analogy between boundary lines of lands and phases of human experience presupposes the more abstract conceptions of an Aeschylus. They might argue that while the shape of the present expression could be cognate with the πείρατα γαίης formulas, there is no reason to think that the sense of πείρατα in those formulas accompanied the technical influence--there is no reason to think that Homeric poetry described psychological extremities in terms of physical space.

The phrase with which Odysseus himself specifies the significance of πείρατ᾽ ἀέθλων answers this objection. The second clause in the lines quoted is a gloss upon the first.

[7]See xi 121-136.
[8]Krause 1936: 148.

That which separates Odysseus from the πείρατ' ἀέθλων is an ἀμέτρητος πόνος, a labor whose dimensions cannot be measured. The integration of the imagery is admirable. Both clauses refer to the journey to a place unknown, and therefore of incalculable distance. Behind this journey lay another, the one to Ithaca, which included many contests and was itself a great ἄεθλον between Odysseus and Poseidon. Yet only with the accomplishment of the coming "immeasurable labor" will Odysseus have conquered the distance between the "world" of struggle, that is, this "world" of life, and the "world" of peace and death. The image of an immeasurably distant boundary line defining opposite states of physical and psychological being aptly portrays Odysseus' fate.

(3) ὅπλ' ἐν χερσὶν ἔχων χαλκήϊα, πείρατα τέχνης iii 433

As with πείρατ' ἀέθλων, it is easy to see the formal analogue of πείρατα τέχνης in πείρατα γαίης, but the problem here is the precise meaning of the phrase. In what sense can tools be the "boundaries" of the goldsmith's skill? Even if the particular signification of "boundaries" is put aside, and πείρατα is interpreted simply as "end" or "perfection", the meaning of the phrase is still unclear.[9] In apposition with the tools, πείρατα τέχνης can hardly desig-

[9]See End-note C.

nate the "perfection" itself of the craft, i.e., the wrought gold.

In order to make sense of the phrase as a modifier of ὅπλα, πείρατα has to be read as a verbal noun, "things which define, or determine". Would the audience of Epic have felt that poetic propriety was violated by extending the sense of πείρατα from "boundaries" to "things which form boundaries", or "things which define the limits of"? Or would they have accepted such a widening of semantic range as typical of the formulaic style?

Such semantic inconsistency is not, in fact, unparalleled in Homeric poetry. For an example, one need look no further than the second word of the formula, τέχνη. Generally in the Epics, it means "art" or "the exercise of art", but it is also employed to designate the "work of art" itself. In viii 327 and 332 the plural, τέχνας, and τεχνῃσι, refers to the chains in which Hephaistos trapped Ares and Aphrodite. The word also serves as an alternate for δόλος, when a word with an initial long syllable is required:

αὐτὰρ ὁ τέχνῃσίν τε καὶ αἱμυλίοισι λόγοισιν
ἤθελεν ἐξαπατᾶν Κυλλήνιος Ἀργυροτόξον·

<u>h</u>. <u>Merc</u>. 317-318

αὐτίκα δ' Αἴγισθος δολίην ἐφράσσατο τέχνην.

iv 529

What Aigisthos contrived was an ambush. The choice of δολίην τέχνην to denote this δόλος was possibly motivated by such usages as

βάλλομεν· οὐδ' ὁ γέρων δολίης ἐπελήθετο τέχνης,

iv 455

where δολίης τέχνης refers to Proteus' skill in changing forms.

In Homeric poetry, then, τέχνη can mean both "the exercise of skill" and "the work of skill", both the action and the object. A similar semantic range for πείρατα is not unique.[10] Technical exigency could have motivated the extension of sense from "boundaries" to "things which define or determine". A poet got as far as ὅπλ' ἐν χερσὶν ἔχων χαλκήϊα. An Adonic segment was required to complete the line. The poet may have remembered a formula like πείρατα γαίης, and by a "leap of conceptual thought" arrived at πείρατα τέχνης. At any rate, conceptualization of the function of physical boundaries lies behind the composition of πείρατα τέχνης. The formula is more than a metaphor such as πείρατ' ἀέθλων, for which an analogical relationship involving the concrete designation of πείρατα

[10]Cf. Nagy 1970: 68: "An abstract substantive defining a given action can come to represent, by metonymic extension, an agent whose primary characteristic happens to be this very action."

is possible:[11]

ἀέθλων : e.g. τέρμα :: γαίης : πείρατα

According to this analogy, πείρατ' ἀέθλων means "the boundaries of this world (γαίης) of contests". For πείρατα τέχνης no strictly metaphorical interpretation is possible. The phrase is an early example of Greek conceptual language.

(4) αὐτὰρ ὕπερθε

νίκης πείρατ' ἔχονται ἐν ἀθανάτοισι θεοῖσιν

VII 101-102

Just as the simple πείρατα γαίης formulas at line-end may have generated the metaphorical πείρατ' ἀέθλων and the conceptual πείρατα τέχνης, so the pattern of πείρατα + verb + γαίης in enjambment in

χωομένης, οὐδ' εἴ κε τὰ νείατα πείραθ' ἵκηαι

γαίης καὶ πόντοιο,

VIII 478-479

appears to have provided the model for the shape of the formula in

νίκης πείρατ' ἔχονται ἐν ἀθανάτοισι θεοῖσιν.

Because of the interchangeability of Adonic segments between end-verse and mid-verse positions, a pattern in

[11]For metaphors based upon a ratio of four terms, see Arist. Po. 21.11-13. Here the fourth term, ἀέθλων, is substituted for the second, γαίης.

enjambment such as:

πείραθ' ἵκηαι #[12]
– ∪ ∪ – ⏓

γαίης
– –

could be used in a single line:

γαίης πείραθ' ἵκηαι
– – – ∪ ∪ – ⏓

a phrase which is the formal equivalent of:

νίκης πείρατ' ἔχονται.
– – – ∪ ∪ – ⏓

Also contributing to the creation of this phrase is the conceptual significance of πείρατα seen in πείρατα τέχνης. Menelaos is willing to arm himself and to answer Hector's challenge to single combat because he believes that it is the immortal gods above who "define" victory among mortal men below. The boundary lines between victory and defeat are drawn from above. As the tools in the hands of the smith are the πείρατα τέχνης, so the gods hold in their power whatever "determines" human success.[13]

(5) ἆσσον ἴθ', ὥς κεν θᾶσσον ὀλέθρου πείραθ' ἵκηαι

VI 143, XX 429

Positioning the noun-in-genitive + πείρατα + verb together at the end of the line permits greater flexibility in the choice of nouns in the genitive than does the

[12]The notation, #, indicates a verse-break: after a word = verse-end; before a word = verse-beginning.

[13]See End-note D.

sequence in enjambment (πείραθ' ἵκηαι # γαίης) or at line-initial position (# νίκης πείρατ' ἔχονται): besides - - or - υ υ, the genitive can bear the shapes, υ - - or υ - υ υ. The combination, ὀλέθρου πείραθ' ἵκηαι, occurs twice in the Iliad and appears to be cognate in form with

νίκης πείρατ' ἔχονται

and

τὰ νείατα πείραθ' ἵκηαι #.

In semantic function, the phrase seems to be another example of the metaphorical application of πείρατα γαίης: ὀλέθρου πείραθ' ἵκηαι looks analogous to πείρατ' ἀέθλων # ἤλθομεν. The full sentence makes it clear that movement toward a physical boundary line is the meaning.[14] The challengers, Diomedes VI 143, and Achilles XX 429, command their adversaries: "Come nearer, so that you may arrive sooner at the boundaries of the land of your destruction." Each hero characterizes himself--or the hostile force he

[14]Björck 1937-1938: 146 fails to notice the metaphor here, since he takes πείρατα as synonymous with τέλος; he contends that πείρατ' ὀλέθρου means "the end that is destruction" just as τέλος θανάτου means "the end that is death". The support he offers from Pindar, N. 7.19 is weakened by the fact that πέρας is an emendation, accepted by Bowra but not by Snell who reads with the manuscripts: ἀφνεὸς πενιχρός τε θανάτου παρὰ σᾶμα νέονται (Wieseler: πέρας ἅμα).

In the one textually sound instance of πεῖρας θανάτου, O. 2.31, (not mentioned by Björck), the use of κέκριται shows that πεῖρας is metaphorical and not synonymous with τέλος. See below pp. 146-147.

embodies--as the line demarcating the land of life and the land of death for his opponent. War makes a single stretch of earth a battlefield, and a battlefield is, for the combatants, like two warring countries, each extending to the limit formed by the clash of its hostile proprietors. Each adversary strains to extend the πείρατα of the land he occupies. Each side strives to back their advance with force so lethal that stepping over the "front lines" will mean destruction for the opponent. The war will be over when one side has succeeded in penetrating to the farthest limits of the enemy's territory and making the "two warring countries" one land, entirely encompassed by what is from the victim's point of view, the πείρατ' ὀλέθρου.[15] To be defeated is to see what was once your land, your source of life and safety, become the land of your destruction, that is, become surrounded by the πείρατ' ολέθρου. The metaphorical use of πείρατα with ὄλεθρος in the context of martial confrontation generates this insight into the essence of victory and defeat.

(6) ὀρθὸν ἐν ἱστοπέδῃ, ἐκ δ' αὐτοῦ πείρατ' ἀνήφθω/ἀνῆπτον

xii 51, 162, 179

[15]Compare Ar., Ra., 1463-1464. Athens will possess σωτηρία only τὴν γῆν ὅταν νομίσωσι τὴν τῶν πολεμίων / εἶναι σφετέραν, τὴν δὲ σφετέραν τῶν πολεμίων.

(7) ὡς δή σφιν καὶ πᾶσιν ὀλέθρου πείρατ' ἐφῆπτο xxii 33

νῦν ὑμῖν καὶ πᾶσιν ὀλέθρου πείρατ' ἐφῆπται xxii 41

ὡς ἤδη Τρώεσσιν ὀλέθρου πείρατ' ἐφῆπται VII 402

οὐ μενέουσ', εἰ δή σφιν ὀλέθρου πείρατ' ἐφῆπται XII 79

In the use of ὀλέθρου πείρατα with ἵκηαι there is no possibility of a concrete denotation of πείρατα as "ropes". The concrete sense upon which the metaphor depends is that of a land's boundary lines. But what of the combination of the same noun-in-genitive + noun phrase with the verb ἐφάπτω? What is the πείρατ' ὀλέθρου that can be "fastened upon" someone? Commentators have concluded that some sort of rope is meant, on the basis of a line in Circe's directions to Odysseus for enjoying the Sirens' song in safety:

δησάντων σ' ἐν νηῒ θοῇ χεῖράς τε πόδας τε
ὀρθὸν ἐν ἱστοπέδῃ, ἐκ δ' αὐτοῦ πείρατ' ἀνήφθω.

xii 50-51

The line is repeated in the orders to the crew, xii 162, and in the description of their obedience, xii 179. The verb δέω is used in each case, but only once is the type of binding specified, and then it is not "ropes" in particular but the general δεσμός, xii, 160-161. To the argument that "ropes" are the most likely material for sailors to use to tie someone to the mast, it may be countered that mere ropes would not suffice to restrain the hero, paradigmatic for his intellectual curiosity, from the supernatural lure of the Sirens' song. Indeed, so seductive, so pernicious is the hearing of ὅσσα γένηται ἐπὶ χθονὶ πουλυβοτείρῃ, xii 191, that without these πείρατα, a man will lose his νόστος, xii 43. These πείρατα must be, therefore, at least as strong as chains. However, the text is too vague to verify either interpretation because the exact nature of the bindings is unspecified. Here πείρατα seems to mean simply, the "bonds", just as a country is "bound" by the πείρατα γαίης. In fact, the sum of these two senses of the word suggests that fundamentally πείρατα denotes not a concrete material in itself, like a rope, but rather anything that binds or defines, i.e., that which forms the limit of the outward extension of anything.[16]

Although these usages of πείρατα with ἀνάπτω do not support the interpretation of πείρατα as "ropes" in particular, they do help account for the collocation of ὀλέθρου πείρατα and ἐφάπτω. As ὀλέθρου πείραθ' ἵκηαι

[16]Several commentators, following the derivation in the Etym. Mag. of πεῖρας=τέλος → τὸ πέρας τοῦ σχοινίου, have held that πείρατα in these examples means "rope-ends". This interpretation is not necessary, and the usage of πείρατα at h. Ap. 129 and of πεῖραρ at XIII 359, where the sense precludes any notion of an "end-point", renders it impossible.

realizes the metaphorical potential in πείρατα γαίης, so ὀλέθρου πείρατ' ἐφῆπται/ἐφῆπτο appears to be a figurative application of the sense of πείρατα in ἐκ δ' αὐτοῦ πείρατ' ἀνήφθω. The phrase means that the "bonds of destruction have been fastened upon" the victim.[17] Without altering the position of any word, i.e., by means of, rather than in spite of, the technical demands of the style, a poet combines the two elements, ὀλέθρου πείρατ' and πείρατ' ἀνάπτω/ἐφάπτω and generates, in so doing, a metaphorical expression of inextricable doom.[18] Precisely because πείρατα denotes not a specific material but rather any "binding", the word is ideally suited to describe not only any concrete bond but also any situation which functions in the same way. Bound to the mast, Odysseus is helpless. Strain though he may, he is powerless to move. Certain concatenations of circumstances can bind their victims in a similar ἀπορία. Then any movement meets destruction.

B. Fundamental Meaning and Semantic Range

(8) οὐδ' ἔτι δεσμά σ' ἔρυκε, λύοντο δὲ πείρατα πάντα

h. Ap. 129

[17]A similar metaphor is employed by Agamemnon at II 111 and IX 18: Ζεύς με μέγα Κρονίδης ἄτῃ ἐνέδησε βαρείῃ.

[18]See End-note *E*.

(9) ἕζετ', ἐπεὶ ᾧ παιδὶ ἑκάστου πείρατ' ἔειπε XXIII 350

It is such examples of πείρατα as these that have led to the conclusion that πεῖραρ is a homonym for "rope" and "end" or "fulfillment". The other usages of πείρατα in Homeric poetry, however, have suggested a basic sense for πεῖραρ which accounts for the meaning of πείρατα in both lines: "that which forms the limit of the outward extension of anything". The word describes a _function_ performed by (1) _boundaries between one land and its opposite element_--between the earth and the sea or the streams of Ocean or the "land" of the dead in Hades or Elysium; between the world of life and contests (ἀέθλων) and the world of death; between the land of survival among one's own people and that of destruction (ὀλέθρου) at the hands of the enemy who strain to make your homeland their own; (2) _tools that "define or determine"_ the work of the goldsmith's skill, and in a similarly abstract application, the "determinants" of victory (νίκης) and (3) _bonds_ that the shipmates fastened to the mast in order to hold Odysseus motionless, and in a metaphorical sense, the _bonds_ fastened upon those in a situation of inextricable destruction (ὀλέθρου). These usages of πείρατα fall into two general categories, one concrete, _boundaries_ and _bonds_, and one conceptual, _determinants_.

In view of these two spheres of meaning, it is clear that these instances of πείρατα in the *Hymn to Apollo* and the *Iliad* are not homonyms. They exemplify the first and second types of usage respectively. In the *Hymn to Apollo* πείρατα is concrete. It means the "bonds" that restrain the infant god.[19] As with the πείρατα that bind Odysseus to the mast, the particular material of the πείρατα here is unclear. The word refers either to the δεσμά (cf. δεσμός, xii 160-161) earlier in the line, or to the χρύσεοι στρόφοι of the previous line, or to both, insofar as it denotes any sort of binding.

The use of πείρατα here seems motivated by the larger structure of the line, an ideal illustration of the aesthetic potential of formulaic composition. By expressing the same idea from two points of view, the poet creates a chiasmus, with a semantic opposition between the formally parallel and contiguous verbs:

οὐδ' ἔτι δεσμά σ' ἔρυκε ⇄ λύοντο δὲ πείρατα πάντα.

a b | b a

A | B

In achieving this formal artistry, worthy of the god of

[19] The force of λύοντο here precludes the translation of πείρατα as "rope-ends". If not "bonds", the verb would require something like "knots". The translation of Björck 1937-1938: 147 appears to reproduce this anomaly: "tous les bouts se denouaient."

harmonies, the formulaic poet was aided by his "Muses" who "remembered" the customary slots in the hexameter not only of πείρατα but of the two verbs as well.[20]

The conceptual sense of πείρατα, on the other hand, is exemplified by the line from the Iliad. The usage is parallel to that of πείρατα τέχνης and νίκης πείρατα. Nestor sits down after having related to his son the "things which determine" each aspect of the coming chariot race.[21] The shape of the phrase is analogous to that of ὀλέθρου πείρατ' ἵκηαι/ἀνῆφθω/ἐφῆπτο. The hiatus between παιδὶ and ἑκάστου confirms the juncture of formulaic patterns.[22]

C. Formulas with the Singular

(1) ἄμφω δ' ἱέσθην ἐπὶ ἴστορι πεῖραρ ἑλέσθαι XVIII 501

On Achilles' shield Hephaistos depicts a peacetime procedure for the resolution of murder cases. The defend-

[20]λύοντο: XVII 318; ἔρυκε: XXIII 258, i 14, ix 29, xiv 283. For Μνημοσύνη, the mother of the Muses, as the creative matrix of formulaic art, see Notopoulos 1938.

[21]It is possible that this use of πείρατα in the context of games carries simultaneously the conceptual sense of "determinants" and the concrete force of "boundary lines" upon which the abstract meaning is based. The delimitations of the race course may have been called the πείρατα. See End-Note H.

[22]A. Parry 1971: 191. See End-note F.

ant offers the regular reparation (ποινή), but the prosecuting party refuses to accept anything.[23] The two men then go to the ἵστωρ to receive a πεῖραρ. The specificity of the description, along with the meaning of πεῖραρ derived from analysis of its other Homeric contexts, leave no doubt about the usage here.

The ἵστωρ is one who "looks so as to know", the stem ισ- being the zero-grade of the root *weid-, seen in οἶδα, future εἴσομαι.[24] In the only other instance of the noun in the Epics, the ἵστωρ makes a visual determination of winner and loser in a chariot race. At the funeral games for Patroklos, Idomeneus suggests that he and Ajax make Agamemnon the ἵστωρ of which team of horses comes in first. It is the allocation of the prize that necessitates the ἵστωρ:

> ἵστορα δ' Ἀτρεΐδην Ἀγαμέμνονα θείομεν ἄμφω,
> ὁππότεραι πρόσθ' ἵπποι, ἵνα γνώῃς ἀποτίνων.
>
> XXIII 486-487

Just as the root *weid- expresses both sensory and mental "seeing", so the role of the ἵστωρ includes intel-

[23]For a discussion of ποινή in this passage, see Muellner 1973.

[24]The "d" of the root *weid- is lost in the future due to assimilation with the s of the future formant and the simplification of the ss: *weid + somai *weis + somai εἴσομαι. Compare *pod - si hom. ποσσί ποσί. Cf. Meillet and Vendryes 1966: 55.74.

lectual perception. In this juridical context, the ἵστωρ is to decide the winner between two moral positions. Here, too, his decision determines a portioning of property, i.e., what part of his possessions (and his possessions could include his life) the defendant will pay to the plaintiff. Not surprisingly, the word for the boundary between lands is used for the ἵστωρ's judgment. The situation depicted here must have been common: a disputed division of actual property is the object of adjudication. What the judge gives and the contestants get (ἑλέσθαι) is a πεῖραρ, both in the sense of a terminus and of a "determination".

(2) τοὶ δ' ἔριδος κρατερῆς καὶ ὁμοιΐου πτολέμοιο
πεῖραρ, ἐπαλλάξαντες, ἐπ' ἀμφοτέροισι τάνυσσαν,
ἄρρηκτόν τ' ἄλυτόν τε, τὸ πολλῶν γούνατ' ἔλυσεν
XIII 358-360

It is probably impossible to solve the mystery of the metaphor in this passage to the satisfaction of all. The precise significance of ἐπαλλάξαντες ἐπ' ἀμφοτέροισι τάνυσσαν has been widely disputed. Because it cannot be proved, the function of πεῖραρ in the picture is clouded accordingly. Despite the obscurity of the image, however, the meaning of the adjectives, ἄρρηκτόν τ' ἄλυτόν τε, and their relation to πεῖραρ are clear. At least they illuminate the usage by certifying what the word does not mean. In addition, the arrangement of the first and third lines exemplifies the manipulation of formulas to enhance poetic meaning. The art of these lines combines with what can be deduced from later instances of ἐπαλλάσσω to suggest an interpretation that is coherent, if not certain, for the metaphor here and in other expressions for equally pitched battle.

Reading πεῖραρ as "end" or "rope-end" is countered both by the meaning of the adjectives and by the fact that translations based upon this reading always imply more than one πεῖραρ. The fact that some manuscripts attest a plural, πείρατα, in defiance of the singular adjectives, is a token of the contradiction involved in taking πεῖραρ as "end". To call a single rope-end "impossible to break or loosen" is nonsense. The adjectives must modify not a point but a continuum. As a result, those who, like the scholiasts, interpret πεῖραρ as "end" or "rope-end" are forced to assume two πεῖραρ's, one of strife and one of war, metaphors of the opposing extremities of the two armies, which are joined together (taking ἐπαλλάσσω as a synonym for συνάπτω or συμπλέκτω) to form a δεσμόν that is ἄρρηκτόν τ' ἄλυτόν τε.[25] The lines are thus reduced to a virtual

[25]See End-note <u>G</u>.

oxymoron of grammar and sense in which a singular word, meaning a single end, is modified by singular adjectives whose meaning would apply not even to τὰ πείρατα alone, but to τὰ πείρατα συνημμένα, the "ends" only after they are joined into a bond. From this passage, therefore, as from all examined before in the Epics, it seems safe to conclude that πεῖραρ does not mean either "end" or "rope-end".

The alternative interpretation of πεῖραρ as a "bond" of some strong material is consistent not only with the adjectives, ἄρρηκτόν τ' ἄλυτόν τε, but also with the verb, τανύω, used in Homeric poetry solely of stretching or laying out something so that it reaches its full extent.[26] Among those who take πεῖραρ as "bond", there are two general accounts of the rest of the metaphor which depend to some extent upon the interpretation of the verb, ἐπαλλάσσω. According to the first version, the verb implies the creation of a knot. J. B. Faesi follows Aristarchus in assuming two ropes, bound together and spanned above the two sides.[27] Others picture one rope in which the gods tie a knot, and then each pulls on one

[26]See End-note H.
[27]Faesi 1865: on 358-360.

end.[28] The latter view is based upon the scholiasts' explanation of ἐπαλλάσσω as a synonym of συνάπτω.[29] W. Leaf, the most thorough exponent of this interpretation, explains that "the word seems to mean literally crossing over a rope upon itself."[30]

The function of the knot, according to this point of view, is left either unstated or somewhat unclear. Leaf claims that the gods tie the two armies to the rope and then pull them back and forth. Evidently the two armies are conceived as being entirely encompassed by the knot and pulled as a whole alternately forward and backward. Because the divinely wrought bond cannot be broken by either side, it "looses the limbs of many." Leaf would like ἐπαλλάξαντες to mean "alternately" (although this would leave him no word for the creation of the knot). His reason for rejecting this translation is the correct and often-ignored observation that the

[28]The fullest account of this interpretation is by Leaf 1971: on 358-360. See also Paley 1871: 22; and Pope's rendering: "These powers unfold the Greek and Trojan train / In War and Discord's adamantine chain, / Indissolubly strong; the fatal tie / Is stretch'd on both, and close compel'd they die." Pope's translation is commended by Clarke 1824: 17.

[29]See Scholia A: "τῷ δὲ ἐπαλλάξαι ἐπὶ τοῦ συνάψαι χρῶνται καὶ τῶν πεζολόγων τινὲς . . ."

[30]Leaf 1971: on 356-360. LSJ record this meaning for the word, but apply it anomalously to a rope-end: "crossing i.e., tying the rope-end of balanced war . . ."

(metrically equivalent) present rather than the aorist participle would be required. The action of ἐπαλλάξαντες, whatever it means, is not continuous.

The participle is most often translated as "alternately" by those who hold the second of the two main views of the passage, i.e., that the metaphor is from a tug-of-war.[31] It is not necessary, however, to take ἐπαλλάσσω as "pull back and forth" in order to construe the lines as picturing this sort of test of strength. Although the verb occurs nowhere else in Epic and only rarely thereafter, later usage does indicate a meaning consistent with the preparatory action of two gods about to stretch a cable of contest. The basic idea is of "changing or crossing something over something else" so that the two overlap like two saw-like rows of interlocking teeth (ἐπαλλάττει τοὺς ὀδόντας, Arist. H.A. 501a18) or arms crossed over each other (ἐπηλλαγμέναις δι' ἀλλήλων ταῖς χερσίν, Plu. Luc. 21.5) or the foot of each soldier planted beside the foot of his opponent along the front line of battle (τοὺς ἐπαλλαχθεὶς ποδί, E. Heracl. 836). In ἐπαλλάττοντες ἅλματα ἐμποιοῦντες ἴχνεσιν ἴχνη (X. Cyn. 5.20) the backtracking hares "interchange leaps" insofar as they

[31]See End-note I.

"cross the foot over" to reach one footprint on one side and then another on the other side.[32] In view of these usages, the phrase πεῖραρ ἐπαλλάξαντες ἐπ' ἀμφοτέροισι could mean that the two gods took a cable and crossed it so that it was over both armies, i.e., that one end was on the Greek side and one on the Trojan. Such an action would have to precede a tug-of-war.

The form and meaning of the first and third lines of the passage support the view that the metaphorical picture is a tugging contest in stalemate.[33] Both lines are overtly formulaic and both picture their meaning. The two parallel genitive phrases in 358, each signifying deadly conflict, provide an initial portrait of two armies warring in balanced destruction. The second of the two, ὁμοιΐου πτολέμοιο, is a noun-epithet combination,

[32]Note also the earliest use of the noun, ἐπαλλαγή: in I.74.4 Herodotus couples it with γάμων as a synonym for ἐπιγαμία, "marriage across the boundary of one's group".

[33]The ingenious rendering of the lines by Lattimore 1951 might be accepted without question were it not for the fact that a crossing cable itself cannot be said to have "unstrung the limbs of many", and thus the poet would have applied to the vehicle of the metaphor an attribute appropriate only to the tenor: "So these two had looped over both sides a crossing / cable of strong discord and the closing of battle, not to be / slipped, not to be broken, which unstrung the knees of many." Most recently, Fitzgerald 1974 interprets the image as based upon a tug-of-war: "These gods had interlocked and drawn / an ultimate hard line of strife and war / between the armies; none / could loosen or break that line / that had undone the knees of many men."

the position of which in Epic never varies. Only once does the adjective, κρατερῆς/κρατερή, occur in the second half of the line, and its position in the first half is invariably before the penthemimeral caesura. The genitive ἔριδος is frequently combined with a preceding long syllable to form the pattern, - υ υ -, that either opens or closes a hemiepes segment:

# ἐξ ἔριδος - υ υ - υ υ -	# ἐξ ἔριδος - υ υ - υ υ -
# λῆγ' ἔριδος - υ υ - υ υ -	# ἀλλ' ἄγε λῆγ' ἔριδος - υ υ - υ υ -
(cf. μοι δ' ἔριδος - υ υ - υ υ - #)	# θυμοβόρου ἔριδος - υ υ - υ υ -
	# ληγέμεναι ἔριδος - υ υ - υ υ -
	# εἴνικ' ἐμῆς ἔριδος - υ υ - υ υ -

The conjunction of the two genitive phrases is a composite of

φυλόπιδες κρατερῆς καὶ ὁμοιΐου πτολέμοιο

XVIII 242

and

ὦρτο δ' Ἔρις κρατερὴ λαοσσόος, αὖε δ' Ἀθήνη.

XX 48

Line 360 is obviously formulaic and equally emblematic. Only twice in Epic does γοῦνατ' occur outside an Adonic segment (XI 609, xviii 212). The forms ἔλυντο, ἔλυσα, ἔλυσαν, ἔλυσε, and ἔλυσεν regularly end this segment. The only exception is one instance of ἔλυσεν (XI 106). The composite shape of the latter half of the line parallels the common καὶ ἐσθλῶν γούνατ' ἔλυσεν and τῷ κε σφέων γούνατ' ἔλυσα. The adjective ἄλυτος appears only in this position and only after ἄρρηκτος, in a formula applied only to other divine bonds: the golden fetters of Poseidon's horse (XIII 37) and the δεσμούς forged by Hephaistos to restrain Aphrodite and Ares (viii 275).

The two parts of the line are bound together by a parallel rhythm and a verbal antithesis that suggest why the warfare of two armies, equally roused, is a πεῖραρ stretched taut by their patron gods. First comes man's pressure to break and dissolve the πεῖραρ: ἄρρηκτόν τ'
– – –
ἄλυτόν τε. The two strong adjectives push forward with
υ υ – υ
tough-sounding τ's.[34] The movement is heavy with the three opening longs, then accelerated up to the central break. But the human effort in its very expression is stymied by the alpha-privatives--the formal mirror of a fact, explained by the relation between these two adjectives and the relative clause completing the line. The closing clause is a simple relative: "a πεῖραρ both unbreakable and indissolvable which dissolves the

[34]Cf. Fónagy 1963.

knees of many". But the verbal play between ἄλυτον and ἔλυσεν, each ending its colon, and the repetition of the
- - - υ υ - υ (in ἀρρηκτόν τ' ἄλυτόν τε) by πολλῶν
(- -)
γούνατ' ἔλυσεν suggests that the relative clause carries
(- υ υ - υ)
overtones of cause and result. It is by being "indissolvable" that the πεῖραρ "dissolves the knees of many", and by "dissolving" the knees of many, it is "indissolvable".

Strength which weakens those straining against it is an attribute that may be applied to the line stretched in a tug-of-war and also to the battleline formed by two armies.[35] If the strain by each army to break through the battleline is equal, the line becomes unbreakable. In thus becoming unbreakable, that is, because of the equal losses each side sustains, this battleline, itself a "πεῖραρ of strife and war", also "breaks" many. A

[35]See VI 6 for the confrontation of two armies as a "battleline" through which each side tries to "break". XII 417-425 offers a similar situation. Lattimore 1951 translates: For neither could the powerful Lykians break in the rampart / of the Danaans, and so open a path through to the vessels, / nor had the Danaan spearmen strength to push back the Lykians / from the rampart, once they had won to a place close under it; / but as two men with measuring ropes in their hands fight bitterly / about a boundary line at the meeting place of two cornfields, / and the two of them fight in the strait place over the rights of division, / so the battlements held these armies apart, and across them / they hewed at each other . . ."

stalemated tug-of-war is an apt image of such equally pitched battle: the activity is paramilitary and a paradigm of balanced tension. With Poseidon and Zeus as the contestants, it becomes an admirable analogue of the two gods' equal rousing of their favorites. The two gods stand both for the two armies and for themselves as the exhorters of each host. The men press forward, the gods pull backward; the effect is the same, if the gods stretch a πεῖραρ that is a metaphor for the battle-line of strife, itself a πεῖραρ as well. The attributes of each πεῖραρ are the same.

This interpretation also accounts for the parallel expressions in Epic of equally balanced battle. In the present passage the πεῖραρ on the battlefield is formed by the ἔρις and the πόλεμος. At XIV 389, the metaphor is elliptical, as Poseidon and Hector stretch "the strife of war" itself:

δή ῥα τότ' αἰνοτάτην ἔριδα πτολέμοιο τάνυσσαν
κυανοχαῖτα Ποσειδάων καὶ φαίδιμος Ἕκτωρ,
ἤτοι ὁ μὲν Τρώεσσιν, ὁ δ' Ἀργείοισιν ἀρήγων.

If the underlying image here is the same as in XIII 358-60, there is no contradiction between ἔριδα, with its connotation of a "press forward" and τάνυσσαν, "to pull or stretch back". Again the point is pictured, here by the balancing pairs of names. Directly following both these lines and those with πεῖραρ, the balanced tension of the whole is ruptured by an individual's success.

The same elliptical usage occurs at XI 336 where μάχη is the object of ἐτάνυσσε:

Ἔνθα σφιν κατὰ ἶσα μάχην ἐτάνυσσε Κρονίων.

Here the image is made even more indirect by the singular subject Κρονίων, but the addition of ἶσα obviates confusion. The line may be translated: "then the son of Kronos made them fight so that their battleline was like a line stretched evenly."

The use of τανύω/τείνω with ἶσα/ἶσον makes the picture sufficiently clear to allow the poet to employ the abstract τέλος, "accomplishment", as a metrical variant for the trochaic πεῖραρ in XX 100-101:

εἰ δὲ θεός περ
ἶσον τείνειεν πολέμου τέλος.

"If the god should stretch equally (or stretch an equal) accomplishment of war" means "if we each should not be able to do more than check the other's advance". In the Theogony the same variation occurs, together with echoes in ἔριδος and λύσις of ἔριδος and ἄλυτον/ἔλυσε in the passage with πεῖραρ:

οὐδέ τις ἦν ἔριδος χαλεπῆς λύσις οὐδὲ τελευτὴ
οὐδετέροις, ἶσον δὲ τέλος τέτατο πτολέμοιο.

637-638

The clause with λύσις and τελευτή is a virtual gloss upon the metaphor since it clearly shows that the line of battle was likened to a πεῖραρ which had to be "unstrung".

The collocation of the ἴσα + μάχη variation of the metaphor with two similes integrates in image the narrative of war and the glimpses of peace. In XII 432-436 both metaphor and simile are portraits of equipoise:

ἀλλ' ἔχον ὥς τε τάλαντα γυνὴ χερνῆτις ἀληθής,
ἥ τε σταθμὸν ἔχουσα καὶ εἴριον ἀμφὶς ἀνέλκει
ἰσάζουσ', ἵνα παισὶν ἀεικέα μισθὸν ἄρηται·
ὣς μὲν τῶν ἐπὶ ἴσα μάχη τέτατο πτόλεμός τε.[36]

The simile at XV 410-413 works in concert with the image underlying the metaphor, since the carpenter's στάθμη is a sort of πεῖραρ. It is a cord that is pulled taut to provide a straight line, either of itself or, when covered with chalk, by the mark left where the cord was stretched.

ἀλλ' ὥς τε στάθμη δόρυ νήϊον ἐξιθύνει
τέκτονος ἐν παλάμῃσι δαήμονος, ὅς ῥά τε πάσης
εὖ εἰδῇ σοφίης ὑποθημοσύνῃσιν Ἀθήνης,
ὣς μὲν τῶν ἐπὶ ἴσα μάχη τέτατο πτόλεμός τε.[37]

36Lattimore 1951 translates: "But held evenly as the scales which a careful widow / holds, taking it by the balance beam, and weighs her wool evenly / at either end, working to win a pitiful wage for her children: / so the battles fought by both sides were pulled fast and even."

37Lattimore 1951 translates: "But as a chalkline straightens the cutting of a ship's timber / in

As the στάθμη forms a straight edge for cutting, so the battle "stretched equally" produced a straight front line where men are cut down.

(3) καὶ δὴ Φαιήκων γαίης σχεδόν, ἔνθα οἱ αἶσα
ἐκφυγέειν μέγα πεῖραρ ὀϊζύος, ἥ μιν ἱκάνει·
ἀλλ' ἔτι μέν μίν φημι ἅδην ἐλάαν κακότητος   ν 288-290

Odysseus is just off the Phaiakian shore, sailing on his raft within sight of safety, when Poseidon, returning from the Aethiopians, spies his prey. Before gathering the clouds and convulsing the sea, he predicts, hysteron-proteron, Odysseus' ultimate escape from the storm-tossed wandering to which the god has sentenced the man for blinding Polyphemos. Fate decrees that despite Poseidon, Odysseus will step upon Alkinoos' island, and with that step, he will have touched the turning point in his νόστος, he will have crossed the boundary between the two worlds of the <u>Odyssey</u>: the sea, raw nature's elemental force, wielded by Poseidon; and the land, where Athena's power will culminate in the act of civilization with which the epic ends. Once landed upon Phaiakia, Odysseus will have

the hands of an expert carpenter, who by Athena's / inspiration is well versed in all his craft's subtlety, / so the battles fought by both sides were pulled fast and even."

broken free not only from the sea's impediments to his homecoming, but also from nature's ultimate bond, the detention of immortality with Kalypso. That bond is, as Odysseus saw, the boundary between undying death and mortal life.[38]

Such is the force which the use of πεῖραρ gives to Poseidon's prediction--πεῖραρ, the boundary between land and sea, between the world of life and contests and the realm of the gods and death (πείρατα γαίης/'Ωκεανοῖο/ ἀέθλων), the determinants of victory or a work of craft (πείρατα νίκης/τέχνης), the bond of rope or chain (πείρατ' ἀνήφθω, πεῖραρ ἄρρηκτόν τ' ἄλυτόν τε), the boundary and bond of destruction (ὀλέθρου πείραθ' ἵκηαι/ἐφῆπται), the judge's determination (ἐπὶ ἴστορι πεῖραρ ἑλέσθαι). In this context the word radiates with each of its connotations.[39] Odysseus will cross the literal πεῖραρ between the πόντος and the γαῖα, and figuratively, the πεῖραρ ὀϊζύος, a phrase which here means simultaneously: Poseidon's judgment of "misery", the bond of the "misery"

[38]Cf. Herakleitos 62: ἀθάνατοι θνητοί, θνητοὶ ἀθάνατοι, ζῶντες τὸν ἐκείνων θάνατον, τὸν δὲ ἐκείνων βίον τεθνεῶτες.

[39]Hainsworth 1970: 97-98: "Because the subject matter is repetitive, traditional art is very allusive. . . . The same is true of the diction. Every use of a formula evokes its other uses, and it is up to the good poet to grasp and make use of these associations." The poet here has achieved this poetic goal by using πεῖραρ in a context that calls up the connotations of the word elsewhere.

caused by both Poseidon and Kalypso, the determinant of that "misery", and the limit of that "misery".[40] As a general term for all Odysseus has suffered before landing at Phaiakia, the poignantly mournful ὀϊζύς is perfect.[41] All that ὀϊζύς includes and why this πεῖραρ is indeed "great" (μέγα) we learn from Odysseus himself in the Epic's central hysteron-proteron, the hero's self-revelation.

The singular appropriateness of Poseidon's words in 289 is a function of the poetic potential of formulaic constraints. Although the singular of πεῖραρ does not occur elsewhere in extant Epic before the main caesura, it is possible to demonstrate how the line's composition derives from use of regular phrases in regular places. The verb ἱκάνει always closes an Adonic segment, and frequently expresses the presence of a physical or

40The translation of Fitzgerald 1963, "the bondage of exile" (with ὀϊζύος rendered as "exile") is wondrously "literal" since, like the original, it evokes both concrete meanings of πεῖραρ, "bond" ("bondage") and "boundary line" ("of exile" from the homeland).

41Compare Odysseus' terminology in recounting Heracles' description to him in Hades as his own god-sent "misery", xi 620-622:

Ζηνὸς μὲν πάϊς ἦα Κρονίονος, αὐταρ ὀϊζὺν
εἶχον ἀπειρεσίην· μάλα γὰρ πολὺ χείρονι φωτὶ
δεδμήμην, ὁ δέ μοι χαλεποὺς ἐπετέλλετ' ἀέθλους.

Cf. πείρατ' ἀέθλων #, xxiii 248, pp. 28-31. The bards' formulaic diction carries the thematic links that inform the nature of their characters by mutual allusion. Thus the Epic acquires clarifying unity.

psychological condition. The length of the subject and object of the verb ranges from a whole line, to (as in the line above) a trochee after the bucolic diaeresis, e.g.,

ἀλλὰ τόδ' αἰνὸν ἄχος κραδίην καὶ θυμὸν ἱκάνει

xviii 274=XV 208=XVI 52

ἅπτετ', ἐπεί μιν ἄχος κραδίην καὶ θυμὸν ἱκάνεν

II 171

ἄσασθαι φίλον ἦτορ, ἐπεί μ' ἄχος αἰνὸν ἱκάνει

XIX 307

χραισμεῖν· αὐτὴν γάρ μιν ὑπὸ τρόμος αἰνὸς ἱκάνει

XI 117

κεῖτ' ὀλιγηπελέων, κάματος δέ μιν αἰνὸς ἱκάνει

v 457

γούνων ἅψασθαι· χαλεπὸν δέ με πένθος ἱκάνει

vi 169

ὃς λαὸν ἤγειρα· μάλιστα δέ μ' ἄλγος ἱκάνει

ii 41

ἄνδρα γέροντα, δύῃ ἀρημένον, ἥ μιν ἱκάνει

xviii 81

In four of its five other occurrences, the genitive ὀϊζύος precedes the bucolic diaeresis.[42] The metrically equivalent ὀϊζυε occupies the same position (III 408). The

[42]See VI 285, iii 103, iv 35, 812.

first part of the line is a composite of several hemistichs:

ὢ πόποι, ἦ μέγα πένθος/'Αχαιΐδα γαῖαν ἱκάνει

I 254=VII 124

ἀλλ' ὄμοσεν μέγαν ὅρκον,

XIX 113

νῦν δ' ὅτε δὴ μέγας ἐστὶ

xix 532

μέγας ἐσσὶ

xviii 217

ἐκφυγέειν κακότητα

v 414

ἐκφυγέειν θάνατον

XXI 66

The rich symbolic significance of πεῖραρ is activated by an expression formed again not in spite of, but by means of formulaic technique.

II. THE ETYMOLOGY:

πεῖραρ and Rigvedic *párvan*

For the purpose of reconstructing the etymology of a Homeric word, the Rigveda is the ideal document in which to find a cognate. It is the oldest of our extensive, literary Indo-European texts, and because of its genre, it retains ancient usage. Divided into ten books or *mandalas*, it is a collection or *saṃhita* of hymns--poems that are prayers made by poets who are priests. All religious discourse is relatively conservative, but the diction of these hymns offers a unique combination of antiquity and regularization of content. The material dates from the second millennium B. C., and each prayer is preserved in the form in which it was included in the collection. Until it was written down sometime near the end of the eighth century, the *saṃhita* was transmitted verbally, but *verbatim*. In contrast to the pre-literate poetry of early Greece, each recitation of a Rigvedic hymn was not a new performance.

As with the Greek Epics, centuries of semantic development are captured in the chronological span of the Rigveda. This historical depth behind the Epics and the Hymns does, of course, also mean that the two texts are a thousand or two years from whatever origins they may have shared. In content as well, they testify to how differently the Greek and Indic cultures developed their Indo-European inheritance. The Hymns, from one to fifty verses in length, invoke and extol the various immortals of the primordial Indic pantheon. Honorific epithets, the divinities' mythic exploits, their particular powers, their past blessings, the details of ritual procedure, petitions for future favors--these are the hieratic elements of which the Hymns are made. Nevertheless, despite these distances between the Epics and the Rigveda, distances of time, place, and literary type, Indo-European linguists have been able, by means of comparative methodologies, to reconstruct for the cognate phraseology of these two cultural branches a common root.[1]

Homeric πεῖραρ has a Rigvedic cognate in the noun, _párvan_, and thus the attempt to form an etymology by comparing the two is not new. No one disputes the perfect morphological parallelism. Both derive from *_per-u̯-r̥/n̥_. The problem for scholars has emanated from the apparently

[1]See Whitney 1873: 1-45, Thieme 1957, and Nagy 1974: 15-18.

irreconcilable meanings that the glossaries attach to the two words. Representing the Hellenists, Frisk notes that *párvan* is a striking formal parallel to πεῖραρ.[2] His glosses for *párvan* are "knot, joint, cut, division". As for πεῖραρ, he believes that πείρατα means "knots" at xii 51 and *h. Ap.* 129. Is there, then, a special πεῖραρ signifying "knot"? No, Frisk concludes, because in XIII 358 πείρατα means "rope" or "cable". Nor does he believe that *párvan* can be reconciled semantically with the πεῖραρ that means "end, boundary". In his *Kurzgefasstes etymologisches Wörterbuch des Altindischen*, Mayrhofer is similarly at a loss to explain how πεῖραρ = "end, completion, termination" can be semantically cognate with *párvan* = "knot, joint, limb, member of the body, part."[3] Each etymologist appears to have accepted without question the glosses provided by the other, an understandable procedure when one has the entire language to cover. Yet the examination of πεῖραρ in the Epics revealed that the interpretation of the word as a homonym signifying both "rope" and "end" is incorrect. The Homeric usages suggested a basic signification for the word (i.e., "that which forms the limit of the outward

[2]Frisk 1960: s. v. πεῖραρ.
[3]Mayrhofer 1956: s.v. *páruh*.

extension of anything") from which the apparently contradictory denotations developed. The question of semantic relationship between πεῖραρ and párvan should, therefore, not be decided without a similar survey of the Rigvedic contexts of párvan.

A. The Meaning of párvan in the Rigveda

In his Wörterbuch zum Rigveda, Hermann Grassmann summarizes the meanings of párvan in the Rigveda as follows:[4]

1) "knots" of plants
2) from the meaning "knots" on reed-plants arises the meaning "reed-stalk" of plants (which is full of pith)
3) "joint" between the limbs of the body, also perhaps assuming the meaning "limbs" (of the body)
4) "knot-point" of a space of time, a projecting "point in time", as "time of festival", "time of sacrifice" or the like (later mostly "alternation of the moon")
5) "tufts of wool"

In his list of the occurrences of párvan, Grassmann gives no examples of the first usage, the "knots of

[4]Grassmann 1955: s.v. párvan.

plants" that lexicographers take as the word's primary meaning. With no instance of *párvan* as "knots", Grassmann's one citation of *párvan* as a "reed-stalk", the usage that arises from the meaning of knots on "reed-plants", comes into question:

> sóṣā́m avindat sá svàḥ só agním / só arkéṇa ví babādhe támāṅsi / bṛhaspátir góvapuṣo valásya / nír majjā́naṃ ná párvaṇo jabhāra 10.68.9
>
> He found Uṣas, the sun, Agni; through magic song he drove away the darkness. Bṛhaspati fetched (the cows) of Vala, who made a show of, i.e., paraded, the cows, like pith / marrow from the joint.[5]

Grassmann's interpretation appears to depend upon (1) his belief that the first meaning of *párvan* is "a plant's knot"; a sense from which that of "reed stalk" might be extended and (2) the assumptions that the plant here is of the reedy variety and that pith is found only in the

[5]Following each quotation from the Rigveda is an English rendering of the German translations of Geldner 1951. His German version is appended here and in subsequent notes. "Er fand die Uṣas, er die Sonne, er das Feuer; er vertrieb durch Zauberlied die Finsternis. Bṛhaspati holte (die Kühe) des Vala, der mit den Kühen prunkte, wie das Mark aus dem Gelenk." Renou 1955-1969: 15.75 translates: "C'est lui qui découvrit l'aurore, lui le soleil, lui Agni: lui qui a refoulé les tenèbres grâce au chant. / Bṛhaspati a extrait (les vaches) de Vala, (ce démon paré) de la beauté des vaches, comme (on extrait) la moelle de l'articulation."

stalk.[6] In fact, nowhere does *párvan* mean "knot"--unless it is in these very lines, for a plant's knot, the point of origin for the new branch, is particularly rich in pith. Furthermore, the context gives no clue as to the type of plant involved. If the reference is to a plant, that is, if *majján* (which occurs only here in the Rigveda) means "pith" and not "marrow", then the translation "like the pith from the knot" is at least as possible as is "like the pith from the reed stalk".

On the other hand, *majján* could refer to "marrow" in bones.[7] Grassmann himself seems to acknowledge this possibility, since his gloss in the *Wörterbuch* of this sole occurrence of *majján* reads, "pith (of bones or plants)". Geldner's translation of *párvan* as "joint" indicates that he reads the simile as a reference to the joint-end of a bone, the nob thick with marrow. It appears, then, that *párvan* in this verse may signify either the knot of a plant or the joint-end of a bone. If Geldner is right and *párvan* means "joint", then this instance should be included under Grassmann's third semantic category.

6 In his own translation Grassmann (1877: 354) renders *párvaṇo* as "Mark aus Pflanzenstengeln."

7 Renou 1955-1969: 15.75 appears to take *majján* as "marrow": "la moelle de l'articulation."

This third meaning, "joint", includes all but two of the remaining instances of <u>párvan</u>. The Rigvedic hymns characterize the joint as the vulnerable source of the body's vigor. Dismemberment is total defeat. The fire god, Agni (cf. Latin, <u>ignis</u>) invoked as the Rakṣas killer, is urged to smash the joints of the magician possessed by this evil spirit:

> ágne tvácaṃ yātudhā́nasya bhindi / hiṅsrā́śánir hárasā hantv enam / prá párvāṇi jātavedaḥ śṛṇīhi / kravyā́t kraviṣṇúr ví cinotu vṛknám 10.87.5
>
> Agni, split the hide of the magician! May the murderous lightning-stone slay him with its heat! Smash, Jatavedas, his joints! May the flesh-greedy beast of prey disperse the dismembered one.[8]

Indra hurls his thunderbolt at Vṛtra in order to sever his joints, as butchers carve a cow:

> asmā́ íd u prá bharā tū́tujāno / vṛtrā́ya vájram ī́śānaḥ kiyedhā́ḥ / gávaḥ[9] ná párva ví radā tiraścā́ / íṣyann

[8]Geldner 1951: "Agni, spalte die Haut des Zauberers; der mörderische Blitzstein soll ihn mit seiner Glut erschlagen! Zerbrich, Jātavedas, seine Gelenke; den Zerstückten soll das fleischgierige Raubtier verstreuen." Renou 1955-1969: 14.21 translates: "O Agni, fends la peau du tenant de sorcellerie! Que la pierre meurtrière (venue du ciel) le tue avec la (flamme d') emportement! / Écrase (lui) les articulations au loin, ô Jātavedas! Qu' (un animal) mangeant la chair-crue, avide de chair-crue, sépare (ses membres) déchiré(s)!"

[9]Reading <u>gávaḥ</u> for <u>gor</u> as per Arnold 1905: 90, ii.

árṇāṅsy apā́ṃ carádhyai 1.61.12

Hurl the club at him in the attack, at Vṛtra, you, the all-powerful, creating whatever exists! Like the joint of a cow, slice him through crosswise while you release the flood of water so that it runs free.[10]

The use of a battle-axe upon an enemy's joints provides the basis for a simile to characterize Indra's action against the violators of Mitra's and Varuṇa's law:

tváṃ ha tyád ṛṇayā́ indra dhī́ro / así́r ná párva vṛjinā́ śṛṇāsi / prá yé mitrásya váruṇasya dhā́ma / yújaṃ ná jánā minánti mitrám 10.89.8

You, Indra, (were) then a clever avenger. As the battle-axe the joints, so you chop up the falsehoods (of those) who sin against the law of Mitra and Varuṇa, as people against a close-connected friend.[11]

[10]Geldner 1951: "Auf ihn schleudere im Anlauf die Keule, auf Vṛtra, allvermögend, was es auch sei schaffend! Wie das Gelenk des Rinds zerteile ihn quer durch indem du die Wasserfluten zum Laufen loslässest!" Renou 1955-1961: 17.24: "A ce (dieu) présente (l'hymne); (Indra) prenant son élan, puissant, (a lancé) le foudre sur Vṛtra, (dieu) qui confère (on ne sait) combien. Déchire (le) comme l'articulation du bovin, de part en part, en incitant les flots des eaux à aller (leur chemin)!" Sāyana provides a particularly precise gloss of this instance of párvan: "párva: parvāny-avayavasaṃdhin", which may be paraphrased: "an alternate form of parvāṇi meaning 'limb-connections'".

[11]Geldner 1951: "Du Indra, (warst) da ein kluger Vergelter. Wie das Schlachtbeil die Gelenke, so zerhaust du die Falschheiten (derer), die wider des Mitra und Varuṇa Gesetz fehlen wie Leute gegen einen verbündeten Freund."

When Indra deals a death-blow to a dragon in a place other than the joint, an a-privative compound of párvan describes the spot:

> átṛpṇuvantaṃ víyatam abudhyám / ábudhymānaṃ suṣupāṇám índra / saptá práti praváta āśáyānam / áhiṃ vájreṇa vi riṇā aparvan 4.19.3
>
> The insatiable, stretched-out dragon, whom one should not awaken, who slept unawakened, who laid siege to the seven streams, (him) have you, Indra, severed with the thunderbolt in a joint-less place.[12]

In addition to harming, Indra can also heal joints that are afflicted. In a somewhat opaque verse that Geldner terms "Berühmte Rettungen und Heilungen Ungenannter," the final miracle is the healing of a broken hip socket:

> vamrī́bhiḥ putrám agrúvo adānám / nivéśanād dhariva ā́ jabhartha / vy àndhó akhyad áhim ādadānó / nír bhū̃d ukhachít sám aranta párva 4.19.9
>
> You, the bay-driver, have fetched the maiden's son gnawed by the ants, out of their shelter. The blind man became sighted, as he seized the serpent. He

[12]Geldner 1951: "Den nimmersatten, ausgespreizten Drachen, den man nicht wecken soll, der ungeweckt schlief, der die sieben Ströme belagerte, hast du, Indra, mit der Keule an einer gelenklosen Stelle zertrennt."

whose hip-socket was crushed came out, his joints healed.[13]

As the joints are vulnerable to disease, so their wholeness means health:

víṣūco áśvān yuyuje vanejā́ / ṛ́jītibhī raśanā́bhir gṛbhītā́n / cakṣadé mitró vásubhiḥ sújātaḥ / sám ānṛdhe párvabhir vāvṛdhānáḥ 10.79.7

The wood-born one has harnessed on opposite sides the horses, which he holds fast with taut reins. The friend of noble birth divided the meal with the gods, growing in all limbs, he has become fulfilled.[14]

Geldner translates párvabhir here as "limbs", and this is presumably the passage Grassmann has in mind when he claims that from "joint", párvan takes on the meaning of "limb". This extension of sense is not, however,

[13]Geldner 1951: "Den von Ameisen benagten Jungfernsohn hast du Falbenlenker aus seinem Unterschlupf geholt. Der Blinde wurde sehend, als er die Schlange anfasste. Der Pfannenbrecher kam davon, es heilten seine Gelenke."

[14]Geldner 1951: "Der Holzgeborene hat nach entgegengesetzten Seiten die Rosse angeschirrt, die er mit straffen (?) Zügeln festhält. Der Freund von vornehmer Geburt teilt das Mahl mit den Göttern, er ist an allen Gliedern wachsend vollständig geworden." Renou 1955-1969: 14.19 translates: "Il a attelé ses chevaux (de flammes, en sorte qu'ils aillent) en directions opposées, (Agni) né dans la forêt, (chevaux) tenus par des rênes (qui les font courir) droit-au-but. / (Agni), bien né, a festoyé (en) ami avec les Vasu; ayant pris croissance, il s'est parachevé quant à ses articulations."

necessary for an understanding of the lines, nor is it supported by the language of the Rigveda in general.[15] The other instances of párvan show that the joints were regarded as points of ultimate vulnerability. Victory and vengeance are defined as the enemy's dismemberment. Health means the healing of crippled joints. The increased potency Agni achieves by sharing the feast with the gods (i.e., burning the sacrifice) would naturally be conceived anatomically as invigoration of his joints.

Furthermore, the Rigvedic word for a limb of the body is not párvan but áṅga, as the following collocation of both words illustrates:

> áṅgād-aṅgāl lómno-lomno / jātám párvaṇi-parvaṇi /
> yákṣmaṃ sárvasmād ātmánas / tám idáṃ ví vṛhāmi te
>
> 10.163.6

> From every limb, from every hair, the consumption broken out in every joint, I now draw off from your whole body.[16]

In this hymn, "Against Consumption", the condition of the joints is again central to the health of the body as a

15Renou's "quant à ses articulations" (above note) indicates that he takes párvabhir as "joints".

16Geldner 1951: "Von jedem Gliede, von jedem Haare, die in jedem Gelenke entstandene Auszehrung, vom ganzen Körper zieh ich dir jetzt ab." Compare the gloss of the Sāyaṇa-Commentary: párvaṇi-parvaṇi: avayavānāṃ saṃdhau, "at the juncture of limbs".

whole.

The reason why the joints are so crucial is portrayed by a simile in the final use of _párvan_ as joint:

> imé mā pītā́ yaśása uruṣyávo / rátham ná gā́vaḥ sám
> anāha párvasu / té mā rakṣantu visrásaś carítrād /
> utá mā srā́mād yavayantv índavaḥ 8.48.5
>
> These honored (Soma-draughts), helpers in my need, are drunk. As the straps the carriage, you hold (me) together in the joints. May these juices guard me from fracture of the leg and preserve me from lameness.[17]

As straps hold the wagon together, so the Soma-draughts prevent the collapse of the joints. The strengthened joints thus become the agents of the Soma-draughts' protection against lameness and not so much "fracture of the leg" (_Beinbruch_) as "crippledness, the inability to walk" (_visrásas_, "slip"; _carítrād_ or _carítraad_ "foot" or leg"). By the power of the Soma-juice, the joints too act

[17]Geldner 1951: "Getrunken werden diese geehrten (Somatränke) meine Nothelfer. Wie die Riemen den Wagen haltet ihr (mich) in den Gelenken zusammen. Diese Säfte sollen mich vor Beinbruch behüten und mich vor Lähmung bewahren." Renou 1955-1969: 9.69 translates: "Voici les (sucs-de-_soma_ qui sont) bus, eux qui font honneur, qui délivrent: comme les courroies (tiennent) le char, vous m'avez amarré en (mes) articulations. / Qu'ils me gardent du pied qui glisse-mal et qu'ils me tiennent-à-l'écart de la fracture, ces sucs-de-_soma_!"

for the body as do the straps for the wagon.

None of the occurrences of <u>párvan</u> examined so far requires the gloss, "limb". In the first passage investigated the word means either "knot" or "joint". In each succeeding case the meaning of <u>párvan</u> seems to be "joint(s)", of a magician, a cow, a battle-axe's victim, a dragon, a cripple, Agni as the fire of sacrifice, a victim of consumption, and the devotee of the Soma-juice. One additional instance from a hymn "To the Frogs" should perhaps be included in this semantic category, but it has so far resisted critical consensus and certainty is impossible.

> yát eṣā̃m anyó anyásya vā́caṃ / śā́ktásyeva vádati
> śíkṣamāṇaḥ / sárvaṃ tád eṣā̃m samṛ́dheva párva / yat
> suvā́co vádathanā́dhy apsú 7.103.5
>
> When one of them repeats the others' word, as the student, that of the teacher, then that (segment) of theirs is as a segment of a lesson, which you utter with beautiful voices.[18]

Oldenberg takes <u>párva</u> here as "joints" and translates: "all das (Tun) von ihnen (geht vor sich) wie mit Voll-

[18]Geldner 1951: "Wenn einer von ihnen des anderen Wort (nach)spricht wie der Lernende das des Meisters, dann ist das von ihnen vollkommen wie ein Lehrabschnitt, was ihr auf dem Wasser mit schönen Stimmen redet."

kommenheit (in Vollständigkeit) Gelenke (dem Körper zugehören)."[19] The Sāyana-Commentary paraphrases: "Your whole body consisting of limbs changes into one with whole limbs. In the hot period the frogs turned into earth, in the rainy time they appear again with whole limbs."[20] The alternate translation offered by Geldner to those who accept Sāyana's interpretation is "every limb on them is then equally perfect, when . . . ." Geldner's own view (and that of MacDonnell)[21] is that *párvan* here refers to a "section" of a hymn which students learned by repeating in unison the lines chanted by their instructor. Geldner points to the simile of the first two Padas as evidence for this translation, otherwise unparalleled in the Rigveda. This interpretation is ingenious and impossible to disprove A closer look at the context, however, suggests that "segment of a lesson" is not a likely interpretation of *párvan* here.

[19]Oldenberg 1909-1912: on 7.103.5. His translation is mistakenly rendered by Velenkar (1963:224) as "all that (action) of theirs is (attended by fulness), just as their limb, i.e., body, is attended by fulness." Professor Samuel Atkins suggests a rendering based upon *párvan* = "joint": "When one of them repeats the utterance of the other as a student does that of the teacher, all this (antiphonal chanting) of theirs (in its completeness, i.e., reciprocal concord) is like the joints (of the body) in their completeness (i.e., the reciprocal concord of their interaction)."

[20]Translation of the citation by Geldner (1951: 272).

[21]MacDonnell and Keith 1958: s.v. *párvan*.

The point of comparison between the croaking frogs and the teacher with his student is only the fact of antiphonal response. The situation in the hymn is not that of a group of many student frogs answering one frog leader. The frogs' song is not the regimented reply of students striving for verbatim memorization of a "fixed text". The frogs are more like jazz musicians, each responding to the riff of another. The earlier verses of the hymn, as translated by H. D. Velenkar, illustrate the song's unrehearsed spontaneity:

> (3) When he, (i.e. Parjanya) rained over them while they lay eager and thirsty (in the dry lake) at the arrival of the rainy season, one of them croaks and approaches another who greets him in return, as a son does his father.
>
> (4) One of these two joyfully greets the other, when both have rejoiced in the downpour of waters, when each frog, being fully drenched in rain, has leapt out and when the spotted one mixes up his voice with that of the yellow one.

In Velenkar's own interpretation of the passage <u>párvan</u> means a "sacrificial session". He translates:

> When one of these repeats the speech of the other as a pupil does that of his teacher, all that (action) of these (owing to its fullness) is like the periodical

> sacrifice in (lit. with) all its fullness, when you of the lovely voice speak out in the midst of waters.[22]

On stanzas 2-6 in general, he claims that "we have an imagery from the general behavior of men of different status and age when they joyfully meet on a festive occasion like the performance of a long sacrificial session, greeting one another."[23] Velenkar might have added in support of his reading the fact that in verse 7 the frogs are likened to priests reciting at a Soma sacrifice:

> Like the priests at the Atiratra sacrifice, reciting around a (Soma-) filled tub, you, O Mandukas, punctually attend on the day of the year which ushers in the rains, (croaking around the water-filled lake).[24]

and in verse 1, they are characterized as Brahmins who keep a vow of silence during the dry period and then at the inspiration of Parjanya break into sacrificial recitation. Taking párvan as a "sacrificial session" would, therefore, accord well with the imagery of the hymn as a whole.

[22]Velenkar 1963: 223-224.
[23]Velenkar 1963: 222.
[24]Velenkar 1963: 224.

Velenkar's rendering is also the only candidate besides _párvan_ = "joint" that can be supported by parallel Rigvedic usage. It has also been shown that "limb" is not a necessary translation in 10.79.7 (the only other occurrence for which "limb" has been offered),[25] and _párvan_ never means "section" elsewhere. Velenkar's reading, on the other hand, is paralleled by the instances of _párvan_ classed under Grassmann's gloss, "point in time".

Two occurrences of _párvan_ belong under this fourth category of meaning. The first is undisputed:

> bhárāmedhmáṃ kr̥ṇávāmā havíṅṣi te / citáyantaḥ párvaṇā-parvaṇā vayám / jīvā́tave pratarám sādhayā dhíyó / 'gne sakhyé mā́ riṣāmā vayáṃ táva 1.94.4
>
> We wish to bring you firewood, to prepare a sacrifice for you, carefully, on every alternation of the moon. Bring our purpose to fulfillment, that we may live still longer! - O Agni, in your friendship may we not come to harm.[26]

[25] See pp. 71-72.

[26] Geldner 1951: "Wir wollen dir Brennholz bringen, dir Opfer bereiten, achtsam, an jedem Mondwechsel. Bring unsere Absichten in Erfüllung, dass wir noch länger leben! - O Agni, in deiner Freundschaft sollten wir nicht zu Schaden kommen." Renou 1955-1969: 12.24 translates: Portons la bûche-flambante, préparons les offrandes pour toi, faisant attention nous (autres) à chaque joint (de l'office liturgique)! / Pour que nous vivions plus avant,

The point in time here is that moment at which one phase of the moon ends and another begins. As in 7.103.5, if Velenkar is right, it is the time of a sacrifice. On the basis of this usage of párvan, the one instance of the compound, soma-párvan, has been interpreted as "the time of the soma-sacrifice":

> índréhi mátsy ándhaso / víśvebhiḥ somapárvabhiḥ /
> mahā̆ñ abhiṣṭír ójasā 1.9.1
>
> Indra! Come hither, intoxicate yourself on the draughts on all soma-holidays, you the great, superior in strength.[27]

The authority of párvan as "reed-stalk", however, has spawned a second translation noted by Geldner, the "soma-stalks". Geldner resolves the two with the possibility of a word-play with both significances. Yet it is the juice and not the stalks that would intoxicate Indra.[28]

mène droit au but (nos) visions-poétiques! O Agni, puissions-nous nous-mêmes ne pas subir de dommage en ton amitié!" In 12.96 he glosses párvan here as "articulation de l'année liturgique", while in 14.81 he gives for this usage the translation, "articulation lunaire (phase)".

[27]Geldner 1951: "Indra! Komm herbei, berausche dich am Trank an allen Somafesttagen du der Grosse, an Stärke überlegen!"

[28]Cf. Renou 1955-1969: 17.5, ". . .enivre toi du breuvage sômique avec toutes les nodosités (de la tige) de soma. . ." which has the virtue of taking párvan as "plant-knot" and not "stalk"; yet, again, it would seem that the filtration necessary to release the juice would separate the hallucinogenic Soma from the plant's nodosités.

"Soma-sacrifice" or "Soma-holiday" alone fits the sense.

Were it not for one final usage of *párvan*, it would seem that the basic sense of the word was to be reconstructed from the two general meanings, "joint" and "joint of time, i.e. time-juncture," and one possible occurrence as "plant knot". One vexed verse, however, where *párvan* seems to mean "tufts of wool", has created Grassmann's fifth semantic classification:

> vṛ́ṣā vṛ́ṣandhiṃ cáturaśrim ásyann / ugró bāhúbhyāṃ
> nṛ́tamaḥ śácīvān / śriyé páruṣṇīm uṣámāṇa ū́rṇām /
> yásyāḥ párvāṇi sakhyā́ya vivyé 4.22.2
>
> He who has the power of the bull, who hurls with the arms the four-angled (club) containing (?) a bull, the powerful one, the most valiant one, the mighty one, who for splendor clothed himself in the Paruṣṇi, (as) in wool, whose tufts he has put on for friendship.[29]

This instance of *párvan* can make no reliable contribution to the reconstruction of the word's primary significance: the stanza is so replete with additional problems and unknowns that any translation of *párvan* here must remain

[29]Geldner 1951: "Der Bullenhafte, der die einen Bullen enthaltende (?) vierkantige (Keule) mit den Armen schleudert, der Gewaltige, Mannhafteste, Mächtige, der zum Prunk sich in die Paruṣṇī (wie) in Wolle kleidet, deren Flocken er zur Freundschaft umgelegt hat . . . ."

ultimately speculative, including the customary "tufts of wool".[30] Accepting this gloss hypothetically and pursuing the verse's puzzles is not, however, fruitless, for it leads to the investigation of an apparent synonym of párvan in párus.

All the commentary on 4.22.2 suggests that the lines contain a complicated play on páruṣṇīm, ū́rṇām, and párvāṇi. Trying to untangle the relationship among the words reveals the possibility of a triple-faceted word-play. The first pun would involve the Paruṣṇī, a river (later called the Ravi) whose name is the feminine singular of the adjective, paruṣá, glossed as:

1) knotty
2) spotted
3) tufty

On the basis of these glosses, scholars have posited several derivations for the river's name:

[30]Geldner (1951) prefaces his notes to the entire hymn with the remark: "Im einzelnen manche Schwierigkeiten." Among the difficulties is uṛ́ṣandhim, an obscure hapax, termed "sinnlose" by Oldenberg (1909-1912: I.286), who suggests the reading tríṣandhi. Also unclear is the reference in sakhyā́yā on which Oldenberg concedes: "Was sakhyā́yā soll, können wir ohne Kenntnis des Mythus nicht wissen" (1909-1912: I.287). As for the intriguing páruṣṇīm, it cannot be determined with certainty whether the word is the name of a river or an adjective modifying ū́rṇām, "wool". For a full discussion of the passage, see Oldenberg 1909-1912: I.348-349.

1) "Knotty, Rich in Indentations"[31]

2) "Spotted"[32]

3) "Rich in Reeds" because paruṣá in its masculine form denotes a reed in the Atharvaveda[33]

4) "Rich in Wool, Tufty" because the adjective often modifies "wool" and assuming that the river's banks are rich in sheep[34]

If the last derivation is right, then there is one word-play in Indra's "putting on" two things that are called paruṣá because each is "tufty", the river and the wool (ū́rṇām) to which the river is likened. The closing phrase of 4.22.2 could then be paraphrased: "he clothed himself in the river, 'Tufty', as in wool whose tufts he has put on for friendship." This proposed pun between páruṣṇīm and ūrṇām depends upon the river's being named after woolly sheep that inhabit its banks. In addition, there may be a play between páruṣṇīm and párvāṇi that depends upon párvan's equaling the noun párus. Geldner claims that there must be "zwischen páruṣṇī und párvan (= párus) . . . ein näherer Zusammenhang oder ein Wortspiel." But does párvan in fact equal párus?

[31]Böhtlingk and Roth 1855-1875: s.v. párus.
[32]Schulze 1933: 119.
[33]Böhtlingk and Roth 1855-1875: s.v. párus.
[34]Pischel and Geldner 1889-1901: II.208-210.

B. The Meaning of *párus* in the Rigveda

The usage of *párus* in the Rigveda suggests that *párvan* and *párus* were synonyms. Like *párvan*, *párus* usually means "joint", and, like *párvan*, it appears in juxtaposition with *áṅga*, the customary word for "limb":

> yásyauṣadhīḥ prasárpatha / áṅgam-aṅgam páruṣ-paruḥ /
> táto yákṣmaṃ ví bādhadhva / ugró madhyamaśī́r iva
>
> 10.97.12

> In whomever your herbs advance, limb by limb, joint by joint, from him you drive away consumption, like a strong man who camps in the middle (between two enemies).[35]

In one case, the anatomical detail is particularly precise:

> yád vijā́man páruṣi vándanam bhúvad / aṣṭhīvántau
> pári kulphaú ca déhat / agníṣ ṭác chócann ápa
> bā́dhatām itó / mā́ mā́m pádyena rápasā vidat tsáruḥ
>
> 7.50.2

> The rash which is on a twin-joint, which covers the knee-joints, and the ankle-joints, may the burning fire drive from there. May the creeping one not

[35] Geldner 1951: "Bei wem ihr Kräuter Glied um Glied, Gelenk um Gelenk vordringt, von dem vertreibt ihr die Schwindsucht, wie ein Mächtiger, der in der Mitte (zwischen zwei Feinden) lagert."

> afflict me with a foot-injury.[36]

In Grassmann's words, _párus_ here means the "joint between the limbs of the body." Velenkar translates:

> May Agni, shining brightly, drive away from here that Vandana poison, which has appeared on a double joint and mounted upon the knees and the ankles. May not the creeping worm have power over me through a wound of the foot.[37]

The phrase _vijā́man páruṣi_ is explained by Velenkar as "that knot-like limb where two parts are joined together, as mentioned in b," i.e., the ball-joint of the knee and the slip-joint of the ankle. Like the usages of _párvan_ with regard to the human body, these instances of _párus_ picture the joints as vulnerable to debilitating disease. And as the defeat of the enemy was described as dismemberment, so the sacrificial animal is to be cut apart precisely at each _párus_:

> Cátustriṁśad vājíno devábandhor / váṅkrīr áśvasya
> svádhitiḥ sám eti / áchidrā gā́trā vayúnā kṛṇota /
> páruṣ-parur anughúṣyā vī́ śasta 1.162.18

[36]Geldner 1951: "Der Ausschlag, der an einem Zwillingsgelenk ist, der die Kniegelenke und Fussknöchel überzieht, den soll das brennende Feuer von da vertreiben. - Nicht soll mich der Schleicher mit einem Fussschaden heimsuchen!"

[37]Velenkar 1963: 117.

The axe strikes the thirty-four ribs of the war-horse that is the associate of the gods. Put in order the body-parts intact; divide them limb for limb, calling out successively (the names of the parts).[38]

Knowing details of cult practice such as how a victim should be slaughtered undoubtedly separated the priests from the laity among the early Indians. Butchered incorrectly, the victim would ruin the ritual. Because the verse above shows that the animal was to be severed at the joints, Grassmann's gloss of *párus* in the following verse, "segment of sacrificial procedure ", appears somewhat shy of the mark.

yám áichāma mánasā sò 'yám ā́gād / yajñásya vidvā́n
páruṣaś cikitvā́n / sá no yakṣad devátātā yájīyān / ní
hí ṣátsad ántaraḥ pū́rvo asmát 10.53.1

He has just come whom we sought in spirit; he is well-informed about the sacrifice and mindful of its articulation. As the better sacrificer may he sacrifice for us in the service of the god. So then may he take his seat before us in the vicinity nearest.[39]

[38]Geldner 1951: "Auf vierunddreissig Rippen des göttergesellten Streitrosses trifft das Beil. Richtet die Körperteile unverletzt her, zerleget sie Glied für Glied der Reihe nach ausrufend!"

[39]Geldner 1951: "Gekommen ist jetzt der, den wir im Geiste suchten, des Opfers ist er kundig und seiner Gliederung eingedenk. Als der besser Opfernde möge er für

Agni's hieratic expertise is defined first generally--he is well-informed about the sacrifice--and then specifically--he is mindful of the joint, the place where the victim must be dismembered. Geldner's "articulation" is closer to the point.[40]

Besides these cases where *párus* means "joint", there is one instance where the word may mean either "joint" or "plant knot".

> índra ukthéna śávasā párur dadhe / bṛ́haspate pratarītā́sy ā́yuṣaḥ / yajñó mánuḥ prámatir naḥ pitā́ hí kam / ā́ sarvátātim áditim vṛṇīmahe 10.100.5
>
> Through praise Indra has put forth in power a joint. Bṛhaspati, you are the lengthener of our life. The offering is Manu, because he is our providence and our father. We beg perfection from the Aditi.[41]

Geldner translates *párus* as "joint" but notes that the image here is taken from a plant. Thus there may be a word-play in the use of *párus* depending upon both

---

uns im Gottesdienst opfern. So möge er denn in nächster Nähe vor uns seinen Platz einnehmen!" Renou 1955-1969: 14.16 translates: "(Le récitant): Ce (dieu) que nous cherchions en pensée, le voici venu, lui qui connaît le sacrifice, qui comprend l'articulation (du sacrifice). / Tel (étant), qu'il sacrifie pour nous dans le service-divin, lui qui sacrifie mieux (qu'aucun autre); qu'il s'assoie tout proche, en avant de nous!"

[40]Cf. Renou's "l'articulation (du sacrifice)", above note.

[41]Geldner 1951: "Indra hat durch den Lobpreis an

meanings. Like a plant, Indra has put forth a "knot" from which a new branch may grow, as a limb on the body appears to sprout from the joint.

The final occurrence of párus, like that of párvan in 4.22.2, does not admit of reliable interpretation.[42] It comes in a verse of Soma-hymn that alludes to the technical processes by which the divine draught was produced.

> eṣá vásūni pibdanā / páruṣā yayiván áti / áva śā́deṣu grachati 9.15.6
>
> This one (Soma), when with the stalk-limb he has gone through (the strainer), finds durable riches in his sprouts.[43]

Kraft ein Gelenk angesetzt. Bṛhaspati, du bist der Verlängerer unseres Lebens. Das Opfer ist Manu, denn es ist unsere Vorsehung und Vater. Wir erbitten Vollkommenheit von der Aditi." Renou 1955-1969: 5.64 translates: "Avec sa force-physique Indra a mis sur lui une jointure (nouvelle) grâce à l'hymne. O Bṛhaspati, tu es le prolongateur de (notre) durée-de-vie. / Le sacrifice est l'Homme, car il est pour nous une providence, oui, un père. Nous demandons-par-choix l'intégrité (des biens, en sorte qu'il n'y ait) point d'attache (avec le mal)."

[42] At the outset of his long note on this stanza, Oldenberg (1909-1912: II.157,158) says, "Viel Dunkles" and candidly concedes at the end of the note, "Ich weiss die Schwierigkeiten nicht zu lösen." Contributing to the difficulties are pibdanā: the two Rigvedic instances of the word yield no certain sense; and śā́deṣu: a Rigvedic hapax, variously glossed as "Gras" or "Abfall" by Oldenberg, "Somagefass" by Grassmann (1955: s.v.) while Geldner thinks it refers to a part of the Soma plant and Renou (1955-1969: 8.64n.) suggests "tranche herbeuse".

[43] Geldner 1951: "Dieser, wenn er mit dem Stengelglied (durch die Seihe) hindurchgegangen ist, findet die dauerhaften Schätze in seinen Trieben."

The most recent and painstaking attempt to elucidate the verse is that of S.S. Bhawe.[44] His results and those of all previous commentators are prejudiced, however, by the fact that all assume the Soma plant to be some sort of leafy, multi-branched plant. No one has reviewed the passage in light of R. Gordon Wasson's identification, accepted by many contemporary Vedic scholars, of the Soma with the fly-agaric mushroom.[45] This usage of _párus_ must, therefore, be left out of account, leaving "joint" and possibly "plant knot" as the range of the word's meaning.

C. The Synonymy of _párvan_ and _párus_

To return to the question that precipitated this survey of _párus_: does _párvan_ equal _párus_? The two do seem to be synonymous, since the semantic range of both words includes the meanings, "joint" and "plant knot". Only the designation of a "joint of time" is restricted to _párvan_. Pursuing Geldner's suggestion of a word-play between _páruṣṇīm_ and _párvāṇi_ in 4.22.2 has, therefore, aided the investigation of _párvan_ because it has led to the determination of synonymy between _párvan_ and _párus_. The glosses of both words suggest a basic sense of "that

[44]Bhawe 1957: I.71-73.
[45]Wasson 1968. For a review of Wasson's theory see D. Ingalls 1971.

at which one thing ends and another begins".

The question now arises of whether this synonymy can in turn shed any light on the phrase in 4.22.2 that led to its discovery. The customary translation of *párvan* here as "tuft of wool" is at least not contradicted by the word's primary significance, "that at which one thing ends and another begins". If *párvan* does denote "tufts of wool" here, the synonymity between *párvan* and *párus* would add two additional levels of word-play to the possible pun between *páruṣṇīm* and *ū́rṇām*, paraphrased above (p. 82) as "he clothed himself in the river, 'Tufty', as in wool whose tufts he put on for friendship." First, because *párus* is synonymous with *párvan*, the verse would bear the force of

> "he clothed himself in the river, *Párus*-ish, as in wool whose *párus*'s he put on for friendship."

The next level of possible punning emerges from consideration of (1) the basic sense of *párvan*/*párus*, "that at which one thing ends and another begins". (2) the meanings of the adjective, *páruṣa*, "knotty," "spotted," and "tufty". and (3) what the river must have done in order for this simile to make sense. If (as Geldner suggests),[46] the

[46]Geldner 1951: "Indra, bez. die Marut, legen sich die Paruṣṇī als Wolle um oder kleiden sich in der P. in Wolle. Das soll wohl heissen: Beim Überschreiten der P. bleibt der Schaum der P. wie Wolle an ihnen hängen."

simile implies that the foam of the forded Parusni clung to Indra as tufts of wool hang upon a skin, the drops of the river, "Párus-ish", function like "párus's", and in doing so, illustrate the fundamental significance of párvan/párus. Thus, the verse would mean

> "he clothed himself in the river, "Párus-ish", whose drops, by acting like párus's, made the river like a sheep-skin whose párus's he put on for friendship."

Each of the three paraphrased puns is, of course, only the product of speculation based upon the unverifiable hypothesis that párvāṇi here does mean "tufts of wool". The only reliable contribution of 4.22.2 to the investigation of párvan is the question it raises for which an answer can be ascertained, i.e., are párvan and párus synonyms? The synonymy itself, however, raises still another question, i.e., why does the language of the Rigveda preserve two forms that serve the same semantic function? Again 4.22.2 illustrates a problem, provides no solution, but initiates further investigation of more revealing contexts.

Why does the poet of 4.22.2 use párvan instead of párus in his verse? If there is a pun intended with páruṣṇīm, would párus not make the point more clearly? Maybe the answer lies in the meter. The statistically most frequent shapes of the verse-type used in 4.22.2, the hendecasyllabic Triṣṭubh, are:[47]

1	2	3	4	5	6	7	8	9	10	11
x	-	x	-,	ᴗ	ᴗ	-	-	ᴗ	-	x

OR

1	2	3	4	5	6	7	8	9	10	11
x	-	x	-	x,	ᴗ	ᴗ	-	ᴗ	-	x

Does the NA plural of _párvan_ fit slots 3, 4, and 5, while that of _párus_ would not? No. The NA plural _párūṃsi_ would fit as well as _párvāṇi_. _Párūṃsi_, however, never occurs in the Rigveda. Here metrical convenience appears to play no part in lexical choice, but formal redundancy of the NA plural is avoided in the Hymns as a whole. Does this verse illustrate the distribution of _párvan/ párus_ elsewhere? Is formal economy maintained elsewhere? And is it chance and not metrical appropriateness that determines which form has been preserved?

A survey of the other occurrences of _párvan_ and _párus_ reveals no redundancy in the distribution of declensional cases. There are no formal doublets, except G./Ab. _páruṣas_ vis-a-vis Ab. _párvaṇo_. _Páruṣas_ never occurs as an ablative, however, so that functional economy is unimpaired. The metrical picture is not so uniform. With

[47] Arnold 1905: 11-13.

one certain and three possible exceptions (including 4.22.2), the form used fits the statistically most frequent shape of the meter in question and the alternate form would not. (See Appendix B: Metrical Distribution of _párvan_ and _párus_ in the Rigveda). This formal and metrical distribution of _párvan_ and _párus_ suggests a suppletive declension of the following root + derivational suffix forms.

	Singular	Plural
NA	párus	párvāṇi/párva
G	páruṣaṣ	
I	páruṣā	parvabhir
L	páruṣi	párvasu

Ab. párvaṇo (páruṣas, not used)

The existence of Old High German _faro - farawēr_, "buntfarbig", (cf. _páruṣa_, "knotig", "bunt", "flockig") suggests that this complementation of derivational suffixes is original.[48]

Metrical suitability seems to have influenced the preservation of those forms which fit the most frequent

[48]This parallel is cited by Wackernagel (1905: I.2.491).

rhythmic pattern. In eight of the thirteen such cases, the alternate form would have the same number of syllables. It is rather by virtue of the quantity of the first syllable that the word conforms to the meter:

párur ⏑ –	vs.	párva – ⏑
páruṣas ⏑ ⏑ – (C)	vs.	párvaṇas – ⏑ – (C)
páruṣi ⏑ ⏑ ⏑	vs.	parvaṇi – ⏑ ⏑
párvasu – ⏑ ⏑	vs.	páruṣṣu ⏑ – ⏑
párvāṇi – – ⏑	vs.	párūṃṣi ⏑ – ⏑
párvaṇi-parvaṇi – ⏑ ⏑ – ⏑ ⏑	vs.	páruṣi-paruṣi ⏑ ⏑ ⏑ ⏑ ⏑ ⏑
párus-paruḥ ⏑ – ⏑ ⏑	vs.	párva-parva – ⏑ – ⏑
párvaṇā-parvaṇā – ⏑ – – ⏑ –	vs.	páruṣā-paruṣā ⏑ ⏑ – ⏑ ⏑ –

The forces of metrical regularization, i.e., the desire to use a word of a definite quantitative pattern, appear (contrary to the evidence of 4.22.2 above) to have been strong enough to preserve *párvan/párus* in the Rigveda at the suppletive stage, i.e., to prevent the generalization of a complete declension of forms from one word or the other.

Both the Rigveda and the Homeric poems present parallels to this sort of suppletive declension, but with more formal redundancy than is found in the attestations of *párvan/párus*. By force of their metrical function, the Homeric hexameter has retained γόνυ/γούνατος, γούνατα, γούνασι and δόρυ/δούρατος, δούρατι, δούρατα, δούρασι, beside γουνός, γοῦνα, γούνων, and δουρός, δουρί, δοῦρε, δοῦρα, δούρων, δούρεσσι. The Rigveda contains dhánus/dhánvan in the following distribution:[49]

	Singular	Plural
NA	dhánus/dhánva	dhánvāni/dhánva
I	dhánvanā	
A/G	dhánvanas	
L	dhánvan	dhánvasu

D. The Etymology of párvan/párus and πεῖραρ

If "that at which one thing ends and another begins" is a correct paraphrase of the basic semantic function illustrated by every example of párvan/párus, then it would seem that párvan is, in fact, a semantic as well as a morphological cognate of πεῖραρ. The fundamental meaning underlying the Homeric usages of πεῖραρ is "that which forms the limit of the outward extension of anything". Both párvan and πεῖραρ mark a physical ending. Together these basic significations of párvan and πεῖραρ

[49] Burrow 1955: 226

suggest an original deverbative noun, *per-us/ u^r/n, formed upon the verbal root *per, as it appears in the sense of "to go to the end point, to go over to the other side".[50]

There is ample evidence of primary forms of verbal *per with a goal-oriented signification. Indeed, on the basis of these cognate verbal usages (plus Greek πόρος, πορθμός, εὔπορος and Latin portus, originally of the sea, as the old sea-god Portunus testifies), Benveniste has concluded that "*per- se dit avant tout du fait de 'traverser l'eau'; de passer d'un bord a l'autre".[51] The primary forms of the root are Vedic par (piparti), Avestan par, and Greek περάω, πέρνημι, and πείρω. The occurrences of each include examples of movement to an end point or line that demarcates separate physical or existential modes.

AVESTAN: Several usages of par compounded with fra- signify a passage to a point where a new life

[50]The following proposal counters the classification by Pokorny (1954: 810-811) of πεῖραρ and párvan among the derivatives of the pre-positional-adverbial form of the root *per, i.e., the locative of a root-noun, "das Hinausführen über". Chantraine (1955: 218-219) describes πεῖραρ as deverbative and classes it under the type that includes εἶδαρ < *ἐδ-Ϝ-r̥, cf. ἔδ-ω and εἶλαρ < *ἐλ-Ϝ-r̥, cf. εἴλω, ἔλσα.

[51]Benveniste 1955: 36f.

commences.[52]

Y.46.10 - Forward with all these (faithful few) I (Zarathustra) shall go across the bridge of Judgment.[53]

V.7.52 - Hail here to you, O man (who have entered Paradise), who from out of an existence full of dangers have crossed over here to a life free of dangers.[54]

Y.71.6 - You (O Zarathustra) shall cause the soul to go forward across the bridge of Judgment.[55]

Y.19.6 - Even three times shall I (Ahura Mazda) cause his soul to go forward across the bridge of the best existence.[56]

Avestan also attests a noun, para, m. derived from par which serves a semantic function similar to that of

[52]The English translations have been made by me, under the direction of Professor Samuel D. Atkins. The Avestan phrases cited by Bartholomae (1904: s.v. par) are appended in the succeeding notes.

[53]"frō tāiš vīspāiš činvatō frafrā pərətūm." Note here and in Y.71.16 and Y.19.6 below, the cognate accusative, pərətūm, of pṛtu-, an abstract in -tu- from par, the "bridge" (i.e., "that which goes over to the other side") which the soul must cross after death.

[54]"ušta iθa tē narə yō iθyejaŋhatat̰ hača aŋhaot̰ aiθyejaŋhəm ahūm ā frafrā."

[55]"frapārayā̊ŋhe urvānəm tarō činvatō pərətūm."

[56]"θriščit̰ tarō pərətūmčit̰ hē urvānəm vahištəm ahūm frapārayeni."

πεῖραρ: "shore (of river or sea), boundary, end."

VEDIC: The primary meaning of par in the Rigveda is to convey someone over dangers to the point of safety, over water to the opposite shore.

9.73.1d - The ships of truth have transported the good man.[57]

1.97.8ab - (To Agni) Bring us across to safety as with a ship over the stream.[58]

1.140.12acd - Grant, Agni, to our chariot and house a ship...which may convey across our men and our pay-masters.[59]

8.16.11abc - As transporter, may Indra, much-invoked, carry us across safely by ship past all enmities.[60]

[57] "Śrákve drapsásya dhámataḥ sám asvarann / ṛtásya yónā sám aranta nā́bhayaḥ / trī́n sá mūrdhnó ásuraś cakra ārábhe / satyásya nā́vaḥ sukṛ́tam apīparan."

[58] "sá naḥ síndhum iva nāváyā́ / áti parṣā svastáye / ápa naḥ śóśucad aghám."

[59] "ráthāya nā́vam utá no gṛhā́ya / nítyāritrām padvátīm rāsy agne / asmā́kaṃ vī́rā́m̐ utá no maghóno / jánāṃś ca yā́ pāráyāc chárma yā́ ca."

[60] "sá naḥ páprih pārayāti / svastí nāvā́ puruhūtáḥ / índro víśvā áti dvíṣaḥ." Note the word-play between the

2.15.5ab - (To Indra) He brought the great stream to a standstill in its course; he brought the non-swimmers safely across.[61]

4.30.17abc - Also Turvaśa and Yadu, who were both not swimmers, the master of power, Indra, has expertly carried across to safety.[62]

1.174.9cd - (To Indra) If you can cross the sea, O hero, so convey Turvasa and Yadu across safely.[63]

2.33.3c - (To Rudra) Convey us safe and sound to the termination of distress.[64]

underlined subject and verb.

61"sá īm mahī́ṃ dhúnim étor aramṇāt / só asnātṝ́n apārayat svastí / tá utsnā́ya rayím abhí prá tasthuḥ / sómasya tā́ máda índraś cakāra."

62"utá tyā́ turváśāyádū / asnātā́rā śácīpátiḥ / índro vidvā́m̐ apārayat."

63"tváṃ dhúnir indra dhúnimatīr / ṛṇór apáḥ sīrā́ ná srávantīḥ / prá yát samudrám áti śū́ra párṣi / pāráyā turváśaṃ yáduṃ svastí."

64"śréṣṭho jātásya rudra śriyā́si / tavástamas tavásāṃ vajrabāho / párṣi ṇaḥ pārám áṃhasaḥ svastí / víśvā abhī̀tī rápaso yuyodhi."

7.60.12c - (To Mitra and Varuṇa) Take us safe across all difficulties.[65]

6.4.8b - Now, O Agni, ...convey us across out of trouble.[66]

7.70.2bc - (To the Aśvins) ...the Gharma drink-offering has been heated at the house of the human (worshipper), (the offering) which carries you across oceans and rivers ...[67]

The Rigveda also preserves an adjective derived from par, pārá, "leading, conveying over to the other side", which functions in the neuter as a noun, "the opposite shore of the sea or river, the boundary opposite, the farthest end of a road or path, the end of a labor, the farthest boundary".

65 "iyáṃ deva puróhitir yuvábhyāṃ / yajñéṣu mitrāvaruṇāv akāri / víśvāni durgā́ pipṛtaṃ tiró no / yūyám pāta svastíbhiḥ sádā naḥ."

66 "nū́ no agne 'vṛkébhih svastí / véṣi rāyáḥ pathíbhiḥ párṣy áṃhaḥ / tā́ sūríbhyo gṛṇaté rāsi sumnám / mádema śatáhimāḥ suvī́rāḥ."

67 "síṣakti sā́ vāṃ sumatíś cániṣṭhā / átāpi gharmó mánuṣo duroṇé / yó vāṃ samudrā́n saritaḥ píparty / étagvā cin ná suyújā yujānáḥ."

GREEK:

πείρω - The Homeric usage of the verb indicates that its basic sense is "to go through to the other side, to the end".

(1) "to pierce through"

e.g. μίστυλλόν τ' ἄρα τἆλλα καὶ ἀμφ' ὀβελοῖσι ἔπειραν

(*passim*)

(2) "to cross the sea"

e.g. παννυχίη μὲν ῥ' ἥ γε καὶ ἠῶ πεῖρε κέλευθον

(ii 434)

ἀνδρῶν τε πτολέμους ἀλεγεινά τε κύματα πείρων

(*passim*)

The collocation of πτολέμους and πείρων is reminiscent of the Vedic use of *par*, "to cross over dangers to safety".

περάω - "to traverse, penetrate, pierce"

πέρνημι "to sell," i.e., "to carry across the sea to a foreign market"[68]

[68]Pokorny (1954: 810-811) lists πέρνημι under a distinct **per* root meaning "to sell", although he admits that it is "eigentlich zum Verkauf hinüberbringen". Benveniste (1955: 36f.) treats it as a primary form of **per*, "to go from one bank to another".

ETYMOLOGY:

verbal root **per*, "to go to the end point, to go over to the other side"

> **per-u̯s/ u̯r̥/n̥*, "that which goes to the end"

párvan/párus

"that at which one thing ends (and another begins)"

1) plant knot?
2) joint
3) joint of time

πεῖραρ

"that which limits the outward extension of anything"

Concrete

boundary line

bond

Conceptual

determinant

III. FROM FORMULAIC TO LITERARY ART: πεῖραρ in Archaic Poetry

One act, the use of writing to record monumental creations like the Iliad and the Odyssey, initiated the transformation of Greek poetry from "winged words" to literary property.[1] Through the permanence of the written word, what would have been an evanescent performance became a poet's personal and permanent possession, even if, as in the case of the Epics, the style of the work still typified that of pre-literate poetry, configurations of formulas in an art-language owned in common by all bards.

The evolution from formulaic to literary artistry was gradual, but it is perceptible, nonetheless, in the mutation of stylistic properties exemplified by πεῖραρ in Archaic poetry. It is not the basic sense of the word that changes in this period. Each poet utilizes either "boundary lines" or "determinants". The pattern of usage displayed is not one of semantic innovation.

[1]For example, cf. Theognis 19-30 and the speculations by Young (1961: X-XI) on the possible historical background of the lines. For bibliography on these mysterious verses, see Campbell 1967: 347-348.

Instead, we see a development from relative dependency in the Hesiodic poems upon the Homeric meanings and formal arrangements, to free manipulation and combination by Pindar of all aspects of the Epic inheritance. Steadily from Archilochos onward, the phrases with πεῖραρ become more and more abstract, as the Homeric construction of πεῖραρ/πείρατα with a noun in the genitive (e.g., πείρατα τέχνης) is recreated with complementary nouns of increasingly metaphysical force.

This linear sequence of stylistic development from the Epics is interrupted and qualified by the two uses of πεῖραρ in the poetry of Alkaios. One is an example of the independently inherited lyric formulas posited by Nagy. Side by side in the work of Alkaios with the fragment containing this archaism is another instance of πεῖραρ that typifies what we are more accustomed to expect in Lesbian Lyric: self-conscious and ironic allusion to Epic themes and language in order to express by contrasting analogy, new and different values.[2] The archaic and the innovative aspects of the poetry of Sappho and Alkaios are emblemized by these occurrences of πεῖραρ.

[2]Cf. Lefkowitz 1973 for the use of Homeric military terminology in Sappho 31 and Privitera 1967 for similar phraseology in Sappho 1.

Together, the instances of πεῖραρ in Archaic poetry illustrate in microcosm how the conflicting dynamics of tradition and innovation co-existed during the period. In the Epics was the end of the pre-literate, wholly formulaic style and the beginning of written literature. Once begun, this movement from formulae to litterae was irreversible. The usages of πεῖραρ by Archilochos, Alkaios and Pindar point to the new poetic techniques and the individualistic poetic goals that this innovation made possible.

The changes ushered in by writing were not, however, sudden or total. The recurrence of traditional themes and diction is paralleled by the lack of semantic novelty in the usage of πεῖραρ and the fact that all cases of the word are re-creations to some degree of the Epic, or in one instance, an even more ancient Lyric inheritance. The persistence of the traditional content and the oral performance of Greek poetry is stressed by E. A. Havelock who offers the valuable concept of "craft literacy" to describe the situation between the introduction of writing and relatively full literacy: the technique of writing was utilized not by all, but by a few--some, like poets, who saw it as an aid to the composition and preservation of poetry as they had always made it, and some, like stone cutters, who held one of the new jobs produced by this technological change.[3] It is this stage of "craft literacy" that is represented in the Archaic occurrences of πεῖραρ, the stage in which we see a slow and complex development away from formulaic to literary art that is always dependent upon tradition. It is only gradually, albeit inevitably, that the poets discover the new "politics" and "economics," and the potential for personal expression in a poem that is private property.

A. HESIOD

Describing the Limits of the World

Comparing the usage of πεῖραρ in Homeric and Hesiodic poetry reveals similarities and differences that parallel those between the poems as wholes. In the most recent systematic investigation of Hesiodic diction, G. P. Edwards concludes that it is basically like that of the Epics in language and in technique of composition; it differs in presenting a few more phrases that violate formulaic economy and are based on linguistic innovations.[4] The metrical characteristics of πεῖραρ exemplify this conclusion. The Hesiodic poems include a hemiepes formula with πείρατα, formed by means of the

[3] Havelock 1963: 36-39.
[4] Edwards 1971. Cf. Hoekstra 1957, Notopoulos 1960 and Peabody 1971.

relatively late Ionic innovation of the ν-movable; the Epics contain several hemiepes formulas created by this means, but the phrases with πείρατα, all Adonics, are not among them.

With regard to meaning, the Hesiodic usage typifies the particular focuses of the _Theogony_ and the _Works and Days_. The Epics are multi-faceted. They look far in many directions. Accordingly, they contain a range of meanings for πεῖραρ. The Hesiodic poems take a single theme and treat it comprehensively. For recounting the "generation of the gods" and the "works and days" of humans, only the cosmographic usage of πεῖραρ is required, the πείρατα γαίης that defines the mortal and immortal realms. The _Theogony_ and the opening section of the _Works and Days_ are more exclusively concerned with the acts and abodes of divinities than are the _Iliad_ and the _Odyssey_. The boundary line of the world is thus confronted in the didactic poems relatively more often.

Of the five instances of πείρατα in Hesiodic poetry, three exemplify the formulaic features of the Homeric πείρατα γαίης.

(1) Ζεὺς Κρονίδης κατένασσε πατὴρ ἐς πείρατα γαίης _Op_. 168

(2) ἥατ' ἐπ' ἐσχατιῇ, μεγάλης ἐν πείρασι γαίης _Th_. 622

(3) ἑξείης πάντων πηγαὶ καὶ πείρατ' ἔασιν _Th_. 738=809

The dactylic nominative-accusative and dative plural is combined with γαίης and with ἔασιν to form a line-final Adonic segment. The preposition preceding the phrase is familiar from ἐπὶ πείρατα γαίης # and ἐπὶ πείρατ' ἀέθλων # in the Epics. The overall shape of the third line

ἐξείης πάντων πηγαὶ καὶ πείρατ' ἔασιν

is neatly paralleled by

ἀλλά σ' ἐς 'Ηλύσιον πεδίον καὶ πείρατα γαίης.

iv 563

The pattern of genitive + noun + genitive in μεγάλης ἐν πείρασι γαίης recalls πολυφόρβου πείρατα γαίης #, πάντων ἐπὶ πείρατ' ἀέθλων # and ὑμῆς ἐπὶ πείρατα γαίης #.

In the following lines, the position of the plural at the beginning of the line departs from Homeric usage.

(4) πείρασιν ἐν μεγάλοις, παγχρύσεα μῆλα φυλάσσει <u>Th</u>. 335

(5) πείρασιν ἐν γαίης, πρόπαρ 'Εσπερίδων λιγυφώνων <u>Th</u>. 518

The formulaic segment here is not an Adonic but a hemiepes. The phrases form an irreducible unit, ending at the penthemimeral caesura, whereas Adonic schemes, - υ υ - ῡ, in the first half of the line necessitate a trochaic break, e.g.,

\# νίκης πείρατ' ἔχονται
  \- -   - υ   υ - -

\# ἡ δ' ἐς πείραθ' ἵκανε   (cf. ὀλέθρου πείραθ' ἵκηαι #)
  \-   -   - υ   υ --υ

vs. # πείρασιν ἐν γαίης
- ∪ ∪ - - -

πείρασιν ἐν μεγάλοις.
- ∪ ∪ - ∪ ∪ -

These two hemiepes formulas are dependent upon the ν-movable. Their formation seems to derive from a bard's noticing that reversing the order of the words in the old, common type ἐν πείρασι γαίης # would produce a metrically satisfactory hemiepes, if -ν were added to the dative: πείρασιν ἐν γαίης. Once the new pattern was established, any word of the form - - or ∪ ∪ - could take the place of γαίης, e.g. μεγάλοις, a word occurring with πεῖραρ in μεγάλης ἐν πείρατα γαίης _Th_. 622 and in

ἐκφυγέειν μέγα πεῖραρ ὀϊζύος, ἥ μιν ἱκάνει.

v 289

The formation of these hemiepes formulas reflects the way in which the formulaic art-language developed in relation to the natural language: bards used innovations from the natural language to adapt older phrases and thus increase the formulaic repertoire.

In contrast with the metrical variety of the Hesiodic formulas, the meaning of πεῖραρ in these poems is limited to the line demarcating the furthest extent of the earth. More points along this perimeter figure in the _Theogony_ and _Works and Days_ than in the Epics. Besides the streams of Ocean which border the earth, the _Iliad_ and the _Odyssey_ are concerned with only two places beyond the land of life: Hades and Elysium. The two Epics describe these abodes only insofar as they affect the lives of the heroes. The Theogony, with its narration of the births and battles of the gods, naturally deals in greater detail with what lies beyond the πείρατα γαίης. The physical relation between the earth and the rest of the cosmos is portrayed by the use of πείρατα γαίης formulas with a greater clarity than is offered by the Homeric contexts.

Elysium: the Isles of the Blessed

Only once in Hesiodic poetry, Op. 168, is the πείρατα γαίης mentioned with reference to humans, and then it is not the ordinary mortals of the Iron Age, but the demi-gods of the Heroic Age with whom the poet is concerned. The domains beyond our normal reach are partly divine, like the heroes themselves. And it is only by divine dispensation that even the supermen can penetrate to the ends of the earth. In these didactic poems men are less dominant than in the Epics. No hero returns, like Odysseus, from the πείρατα γαίης. The heroes only die, some at Thebes, some at Troy. Upon these, Zeus bestows a heavenly afterlife in the Isles of the Blessed:

τοῖς δὲ δίχ' ἀνθρώπων βίοτον καὶ ἤθε' ὀπάσσας
Ζεὺς Κρονίδης κατένασσε πάτηρ ἐς πείρατα γαίης

καὶ τοὶ μὲν ναίουσιν ἀκηδέα θυμὸν ἔχοντες
ἐν μακάρων νήοισι πάρ' Ὠκεανὸν βαθυδίνην.

Op. 167-170

In contrast to the Odyssey where Menelaos' ultimate bliss in Elysium is foretold while he is alive (iv 563-564), these lines from the Works and Days look back upon the settling of the heroes in islands of permanent happiness as a fate irretrievably removed from human possibility. Although composed by means of the same formulaic diction, this vision of Elysium marks the distance between the Hesiodic and the Homeric views of mortal potentiality.[5] Transcendent achievement, that is, reaching and returning from the πείρατα γαίης, is absent here. Only heroes, long dead, could attain it, and only after death, when there is no return.

The Hesperides

To localize another heaven, the garden of the Hesperides, the hemiepes formulas of πεῖραρ are used.[6] The first instance is especially interesting with regard to the manipulation of formulaic types. The context is the

[5]On iv 563-564, see p. 26. For the vision of the human lot expressed in the Works and Days, and how it differs from the Homeric view, see Beye 1973.

[6]For more of the motifs associated with the Hesperides and the formulas that carry them, see Boedeker 1973.

birth of the serpent who guards the garden's golden apples.

> Κητὼ δ' ὁπλότατον Φόρκυι φιλότητι μιγεῖσα
> γείνατο δεινὸν ὄφιν, ὃς ἐρεμνῆς κεύθεσι γαίης
> πείρασιν ἐν μεγάλοις παγχρύσεα μῆλα φυλάσσει.
>
> Th. 333-335

The existence of the hemiepes formula, πείρασιν ἐν μεγάλοις, seems to have helped the poet with the problem of expressing the location of the snake. The Adonic phrase κεύθεσι γαίης # is frequent in the Epics; its form and syntactic function is analogous to that of πείρασι/πείρατα γαίης #. Never in Homeric poetry, however, is the phrase combined with a preceding adjective in the genitive, as in e.g., πολυφόρβου πείρατα γαίης. To indicate adequately the snake's abode the poet needs not only a phrase for the general location of the garden, the πείρατα γαίης, but also a more precise expression for the creature's underground haunt. κεύθεσι γαίης # comes close, though it is not the γαῖα proper that the snake inhabits. Its home is the "earth" of the underworld or at least the other world, the γαῖα of such places as Ἔρεβος--an ἐρεμνὴ γαῖα.[7] It is perhaps the availability of a hemiepes formula with πεῖραρ, able to fill the first half of the second line,

[7]The ἐρεμνὴ γαῖα is the "Erebos"-γαῖα : ἐρεμνός < *ἐρεβ-νος.

that facilitates the use of ἐρεμνή before κεύθεσι γαίης #. This position before the bucolic diaeresis is regular for ἐρεμνός in the Epics. The collocation of ἐρεμνή with κεύθεσι γαίης in the frequent genitive + noun + genitive pattern requires no alteration of the standard hexameter slot of the adjective. Again the expression is a function, a product, of technical restriction. And the expression is admirably apt. Ἐρεμνή, calling up all the connotations of Ἔρεβος itself, is the perfect adjective to describe the heavenly but deadly land where this serpent guards the golden apples.

This analysis of the formulaic background of these lines also accounts for the use of μεγάλοις in the hemiepes expression. To denote the extremity of the earth, any formula with πείρατα, hemiepes or Adonic, requires a γαίης. That a hemiepes with both words was available is confirmed by another use of πείρατα with reference to the Hesperides. Here the position of Atlas is the main point.

> Ἄτλας δ᾽ οὐρανὸν εὐρὺν ἔχει κρατερῆς ὑπ᾽ ἀνάγκης
> πείρασιν ἐν γαίης, πρόπαρ Ἑσπερίδων λιγυφώνων
>
> Th. 517-518

The hemiepes, πείρασιν ἐν γαίης, was available, but it would have precluded the use of the line-final κεύθεσι γαίης formula. Hence the need for another modifier for πείρασιν to complete the hemiepes.[8] As suggested above, the choice of μεγάλοις was perhaps motivated by such collocations as μεγάλοις ἐν πείρασι γαίης.[9]

The πείρατα γαίης καὶ Ταρτάρου καὶ οὐρανοῦ

In the course of narrating the birth and final resting place of the Giants, the full cosmographic potential of the basic sense of πείρατα is demonstrated. In one of its common formulaic patterns the word helps describe the place where Kronos hid the Giants at their birth:

ἥατ' ἐπ' ἐσχατιῇ, μεγάλης ἐν πείρασι γαίης.

<u>Th</u>. 622

The combination of adjective-in-genitive + preposition + noun + noun-in-genitive following the penthimemeral caesura is familiar from the Epics. The motive for choosing μεγάλης again seems to be the desire to use the

[8]A parallel situation is provided by the use of πάντα to complete the line-final Adonic segment in the description of Apollo's release from his swaddling bands.

οὐδ' ἔτι δεσμά σ' ἔρυκε, λύοντο δὲ πείρατα πάντα

<u>h. Ap</u>. 129

In both cases the choice of words appears determined primarily by the needs of a poet who composes by remodeling and recombining phrases in their traditional metrical positions.

[9]Cf. West 1966: 258: "This curious phrase is an adaptation of μεγάλης ἐν πείρασι γαίης (622), with the transference of epithet not uncommon in such adaptations (cf. on 319). The omission of γαίης is made easier by κεύθεσι γαίης in the preceding line."

traditional pattern. Interesting here is the illustration of the fundamental meaning of πείρατα provided by ἐπ' ἐσχατιῇ, actually a gloss upon the following phrase. Later, the same language is used in the narration of how the Giants assured Zeus' ascendancy by hurling the Titans down to Tartaros (the πελώρης ἔσχατα, 731). Reference to the stationing of the Giants as φύλακες against escape by the Titans from the battlement around Tartaros leads to an elaboration upon this position of outer limit.

> Ἔνθα δὲ γῆς δνοφερῆς καὶ Ταρτάρου ἠερόεντος
> πόντου τ' ἀτρυγέτοιο καὶ οὐρανοῦ ἀστερόεντος
> ἑξείης πάντων πηγαὶ καὶ πείρατ' ἔασιν
> ἀργαλέ' εὐρώεντα, τά τε στυγέουσι θεοί περ
> χάσμα μέγ', οὐδέ κε πάντα τελεσφόρον εἰς ἐνιαυτὸν
> οὖδας ἵκοιτ', εἰ πρῶτα πυλέων ἔντοσθε γένοιτο.
>
> Th. 736-741

The picture here is of three layers, Tartaros, earth with its seas, and sky, one on top of the other and all of equal extent laterally. The composition of the first two lines is particularly artful. By using two pairs of two, the poet can mention both of the earth's constituents: sea as well as land. The order, middle (land) - below (Tartaros) - middle (sea) - above (sky), emphasizes the balanced tension of distances among the parts. Just a few lines earlier the poet has stressed the proportion among the three, for Tartaros is

τόσσον ἔνερθ' ὑπὸ γῆς, ὅσον οὐρανός ἐστ' ἀπὸ γαίης.

Th. 720

The main point here, however, is that the three areas reach horizontally to the same extent. At that extremity are the sources (πηγαί) and/or ends (πείρατα) of each domain (πάντων), one upon the other (ἑξείης). Above Tartaros, γῆς ῥίζαι πεφύασι καὶ ἀτρυγέτοιο θαλάσσης (728). Above the earth is the sky. The use of the two terms, πηγαί and πείρατα, is not redundant. It distinguishes and includes the two ways of defining the border of a body: conceived from the outside in, the border is the source, the place where the body begins, from the inside out, it is the line of the furthest outward extension of the body, the point beyond which that body is no more and another begins. There is one precarious point where the beginning and the end are one. But the beginning and the end are separate concepts, and πείρατα means the latter, as this cosmographic usage of the word confirms.

B. ARCHILOCHOS

"Unwinged" Words, Poetic Property and Literary Allusion

111 καὶ νέους θάρσυνε· νίκης δ' ἐν θεοῖσι πείρατα

When the "winged words" of Epic were captured in writing, the poems became literary property. As such they could be imitated, criticized or praised by any subsequent poet, either by direct quotation, or by indirect allusion. Along with the recollection of the words comes the force of the original context, provided it is as familiar as one from the Iliad or the Odyssey. The quotation may be direct if meter permits; if not, the choice and order of words may be altered. The one example of πείρατα in the surviving fragments of Archilochos appears to exemplify this process. We can, of course, never be certain that Archilochos and his audiences knew the Homeric poems we know. Nevertheless, it is possible that they had become fixed by Archilochos' prime, and that what seems to us to be a Homeric quotation was meant to recall his famous forerunner's usage.

The second half of Archilochos' line recasts the vivid expression found only once in the Epics (and never again in Lyric):[10]

νίκης πείρατ' ἔχονται ἐν ἀθανάτοισι θεοῖσιν. VII 102

That Archilochos made such adaptations of dactylic formulas frequently is suggested by the 3rd cent. BC papyrus fragment (219-221 West) of several line by line

[10]See p. 34.

comparisons between iambic lines of Archilochos and their Epic parallels, and by Denys Page's examination of all Archilochos' poems in which he discusses this Hellenistic source.[11] That Archilochos' words are an allusion and not an inherited, trochaic phrase is indicated not only by the frequency of such echoes among the poems and the strikingness of this collocation, but also by the metrical fault that the poet tolerated in using it.

Perhaps under the force of the customary Homeric slot of πείρατα near the end of the hexameter line, Archilochos chose to place the word in line-final position, thereby separating it from νίκης and failing to observe the bridge between the last two metra, characteristic of the trochaic tetrameter catalectic: – ∪ – ⏓ – ∪ – ⏓ | – ∪ – ⏓‿– ∪ –. Out of the 92 remaining tetrameters with the final words complete, Archilochos violates this bridge only eight other times.[12] Interestingly, three of the trisyllabic words used occur in Epic at the opening of an Adonic segment, as does πείρατα: γίνεται 122.5 and 133.3 γαστέρα 119.1, and κύματα 122.8. In the case of κύματα

[11]Page 1964: 149.

[12]Fragments 106.5; 112.2; 119.1; 122.5, 8; 128.6; 132; 133.3; 134 (ἐπ' ἀνδράσιν, where the proclitic preposition may remove any sense of word break). Cf. also 124 (b).3 οἷα δὴ φίλος and 130.1 πολλάκις μὲν ἐκ κακῶν.

Archilochos again appears to adapt Epic diction. The full phrase is θαλάσσης ἠχέεντα κύματα. Both κύματα and ἠχήεσσα appear in Homeric collocations with θάλασσα (II 144, I 157, XIII 798), and Archilochos has correpted the η of the hexameter form, ἠχήεις, in order to combine the three. As with νίκης...πείρατα, the poet violated his metrical custom in using the Homeric phraseology, and he placed the dactylic words of the Adonic segment at the end of the trochaic line.

Although πείρατα does not follow νίκης directly as it does in VII 102, the force of the genitive preceding the noun remains and is actually enhanced in Archilochos' phrase. Delaying the noun creates a small but suspenseful hyperbaton which also puts extra stress on νίκης, left bracketed by pauses: the first grammatical, the colon; and the second metrical, the central diaeresis. Archilochos' word-order also achieves an artful A B A B anaphora of ν- and θ- initial words which reinforces his meaning. The situation in heaven makes the earthly exhortation appropriate, just as νίκης θεοῖσι parallels νέους θαρσύνῃ.

The cumulative tone of the line thus rings urgent and earnest. This is not a case of ironic recollection of the heroic past to contrast with the mundane present. Archilochos will not abandon his shield today. On the contrary, the usage here is consonant with the context of the phrase in the *Iliad*. The Homeric line belongs to Menelaos as he takes up Hector's challenge to single combat, outraged at the other Greeks who sit silent. By no means the strongest contender, Menelaos puts the other Greek champions to shame by his acceptance of the duel and his trust in the gods. Perhaps Archilochos wishes to inspire a similar courage in troops who feel unequal to the fight, and so he exhorts a general to encourage them with these same words. It may be the sound of sincere passion in this appeal, artfully expressed with some expenditure of ingenuity in the terms of heroic tradition, that led A. R. Burn to attribute the line to Archilochos' last years when, received back into his native Paros, he was killed "fighting as an honest citizen-soldier" by a man of Naxos.[13]

C. ALKAIOS

Archaism and Modernity: The Duple Character of Lesbian Lyric

Self-conscious imitation of Epic, like that exemplified by Archilochos' νίκης πείρατα, has been the customary explanation for all phrases in Lesbian Lyric with Homeric

[13]Burn 1960: 170.

counterparts. Thus a poem like Sappho's "Wedding of Hector and Andromache" (44 LP) is held by Denys Page to be a deliberate emulation of the hexameter's themes and diction.[14] The basis for this account of "epic phraseology" in the poetry of Sappho and Alkaios seems to be only the easy, but perhaps inadequate assumption that the historically later usage is derivative of the earlier. Applied to the relation between Epic and Lyric, this assumption is foiled by the fact that the metrical genres of Lesbian Lyric are, because of their isosyllabism, more ancient in form than the hexameter with its allowance of substitution. An immutable number of syllables characterizes the Indo-European verse-types inherited by Greek, Vedic Sanskrit and Slavic, while the substitution, ∪∪ = –, is an innovation of Greek.[15]

[14]Page 1955: 65-74. Although he notes that the poem contains motifs that have no Epic precedent and cautiously questions whether poets adopted Epic meter and themes to add dignity to all their marriage-songs, Page assumes throughout his discussion that 44 is one of Sappho's "Abnormal" poems, i.e., one containing Epic forms as a result of the imitation of Epic meter. The same assumption underlies the discussion of 44 by Kirkwood (1974: 142-146). Longo (1963-1964) takes all "epic" forms as "Homerisms". Lanata (1966), too, assumes that deliberate adaptation of the Epics is the source of all Homeric diction in Sappho. The work of all these scholars is rich in detailed parallels between Epic and Lyric that can aid further efforts to determine the admixture in Lesbian poetry of Epic imitation and phraseology inherited by both Epic and Lyric.

[15]See Meillet 1923 and West 1973b.

This historical relationship between Lyric and Epic meter has led Gregory Nagy to posit that the hexameter is derived from isosyllabic verse forms and that early hexameter poets composed their lines with inherited lyric formulas.[16] If correct, this hypothesis implies that the Aeolic poetry from the turn of the 7th century may not be so stylistically uniform as is assumed by the ascription of all "epic phrases" to Epic imitation. Late compositions in ancient metrical genres may reveal ἄλλοτε ἄλλον, both deliberate allusions to the "old" Epics and phrases inherited from a still older lyric tradition.

The instances of πεῖραρ in the poetry of Alkaios provide an ideal chance to test Nagy's hypothesis. Comparison with Rigvedic párvan certifies that πεῖραρ is an Indo-European inheritance. Alkaios uses the word twice, each time in an isosyllabic meter, the Asclepiadean, each time in the plural, and each time in the concrete sense of the word current in the Epics, the πείρατα γαίης. Upon examination each usage illustrates one of the two stylistic properties predictable for Aeolic lyric by Nagy's hypothesis: (1) self-conscious Epic imitation and (2) an ancient lyric formula, inherited not only by Alkaios but also by epic poets who accommodated it to the

[16]Nagy 1974: 37-102.

hexameter.

At first glance, however, it would seem that no instance of πεῖραρ in Alkaios' poetry could support Nagy's theory. The customary treatment in Lesbian poetry of the consonant group, -ρϝ-, is simply to drop the ϝ without compensatory lengthening of the previous vowel or gemination of the previous consonant.[17] Any form of *περ-ϝαρ in Alkaios' poetry would therefore be of a different metrical shape from any instance of πεῖραρ in the Epics. The first syllable of the Lesbian form would be short (Lesbian *περαρ υ υ vs. Epic πεῖραρ - υ). Thus no word group with *περ-ϝαρ in Alkaios' Asclepiads could be cognate with a πεῖραρ formula in Epic.

Alkaios' poem in honor of his brother's return from mercenary service in Babylon reflects this difference between Lesbian and Homeric dialect.

ἦλθες ἐκ περάτων γᾶς ἐλαφαντίναν
λάβαν τῶ ξίφεος χρυσοδέτον ἔχων. Z 27

Here the word order of ἐκ περάτων γᾶς is reminiscent of the many hexameter phrases in which a preposition is coupled with πείρατα γαίης. There is even a case in the Epics of this formula-type with a form of ἦλθον, Odysseus' words to Penelope:

[17] See Hamm 1958: 18.13.

ὦ γύναι, οὐ γάρ πω πάντων ἐπὶ πείρατ' ἀέθλων

ἤλθομεν.

xxiii 248-249

But the dropping of ϝ evident in ἐκ περάτων γᾶς certifies that the phrase is not an inherited formula for this spot in the Asclepiadean line. The inherited scansion of the genitive plural of *περ-ϝαρ is - υ -. This phrase, ἐκ περάτων γᾶς, is a creation of a Lesbian poet for whom *περϝαρ had become *περαρ. The scansion of the genitive plural here, περάτων, is υ υ -. In view of the close resemblance between Alkaios' phrase and the frequent Homeric collocation, it is likely that the Lyric poet is here imitating his Epic predecessors.

An Epic allusion, in a mildly sardonic tone, would accord well with the rest of the poem. After a lacuna at the end of the first two lines, the poet continues:

ἄεθλον μέγαν, εὐρύσαο δ' ἐκ πόνων

κτέννais ἄνδρα μαχαίταν βασιληίων

παλάσταν ἀπυλείποντα μόναν ἴαν

παχέων ἀπὺ πέμπων.

Although the text is restored from ἄεθλον to κτένναις on the basis of Strabo's introductory words to his citation of the poem, the point of Alkaios' accolade is clear. Antimenidas has slain an adversary of "epic proportions". Perhaps the "gold-bound ivory haft of his sword" was a γέρας of the sort given to Homeric heroes after the enemy city was captured. Perhaps Strabo was repeating Alkaios' choice of words in ἄεθλον which in this context would carry its Homeric associations, particularly with Odysseus' combats, hardships,and prizes. But this prize is given not by an Agamemnon or an Achilles but by a barbarian who wins with the aid of Greeks! The struggle is not for Greek glory either in self-defense, in expansionistic adventure, or in funeral games. The recipient is not a hero, but a mercenary who evidently can achieve ἀρετή only in this "mock-epic" manner. And Babylon to Alkaios is not the πείρατα γαίης. This poem is in content not traditional as is, for example, Sappho's "Wedding of Hector and Andromache". It is an individual lyric, self-conscious and psychologically subtle, and it achieves its effect by ironic allusion to Epic.

Epic imitation has also been customarily ascribed to the fragment containing the second of Alkaios' uses of πεῖραρ, but on purely linguistic grounds. This two-line fragment happens to contain the only two deviations in Lesbian Lyric from the usual dropping of digamma with no compensatory lengthening.

ὄρνιθες τίνες οἶδ' Ὠκεάνω γᾶς ἀπὺ πειράτων
ἦλθον πανέλοπες ποικιλόδειροι τανυσίπτεροι; Z 21

Both πειράτων and ποικιλόδειροι bear so-called "Ionic"

lengthening and appear as they would in Homeric verse. As a result Eva-Maria Hamm accounts for them as "epic constituents", appropriated by Alkaios because his dialectical forms would not fit his meter.[18]

This interpretation, although not demonstrably incorrect, is not the only one possible nor, perhaps, the most likely. The opposite situation may be true. The lines may contain traditional phraseology inherited from the period before digamma was dropped. At any rate the fact is that Lesbian Lyric could preserve an inherited formula with πεῖραρ only if the form of the word <u>appeared</u> to be "Epic", i.e., if the first syllable were long. Only this so-called Epic form of πεῖραρ is capable of testing Nagy's theory of the origins of the hexameter. Upon investigation the relationship between this instance of πεῖραρ and the usage of the word in Homeric formulas turns out to be as Nagy's hypothesis would predict.

Nagy supports his etymology of the hexameter with an analysis of the two phrases, the Homeric κλέος ἄφθιτον ἔσται # and the Sapphic κλέος ἄφθιτον #. The formulaic relationship between these two phrases is precisely that between the Epic ἐπὶ πείρατα γαίης # and Alkaios' ἀπὺ πειράτων #. Both ἀπὺ πειράτων # and κλέος ἄφθιτον # occur

[18]Hamm 1958: 18.13 and 41.87.

at the end of metrical patterns formed by the internal expansion of a glyconic metron (= ⏓ ⏓ - ᴗ ᴗ - ᴗ -), abbreviated by Snell as gl.[19] The pentameter of Sappho 44, in which κλέος ἄφθιτον appears, is a glyconic, expanded internally by two dactyls (- ᴗ ᴗ - ᴗ ᴗ). The abbreviation for this pentameter, according to the notation of Snell, is gl^{2d}. The meter of Alkaios' fragment Z 21 is the Greater Asclepiadean, a glyconic expanded internally by two choriambs (- ᴗ ᴗ - - ᴗ ᴗ -), or gl^{2c}. Both κλέος ἄφθιτον # and ἀπὺ πειράτων # constitute partial glyconic formulas of the shape, ᴗ ᴗ - ᴗ - #:

<u>The pentameter of Sappho 44</u>

gl^{2d}: ⏓ ⏓ - ᴗ ᴗ - ᴗ ᴗ - [ᴗ ᴗ - ᴗ - = κλέος ἄφθιτον
dactyls, 2d

<u>The Greater Asclepiadean of Alkaios Z 21</u>

gl^{2c}: ⏓ ⏓ - ᴗ ᴗ - - ᴗ ᴗ - - [ᴗ ᴗ - ᴗ - = ἀπὺ πειράτων
choriambs, 2c

The formula ἀπὺ πειράτων may be described as Nagy terms κλέος ἄφθιτον, i.e., "an independent formula built into the end of a gl^{2d} (or gl^{d} or gl)".[20]

Similarly, because ἐπὶ πείρατα γαίης # and κλέος

[19] Snell 1962: 2,3, 34-38.
[20] Nagy 1974: 133.

ἄφθιτον ἔσται # are both formulas occurring at the end of the Epic hexameter, Nagy's description of κλέος ἄφθιτον ἔσται # designates ἐπὶ πείρατα γαίης # as well, i.e., "a formula built into the end of a (∧) pher^d".[21] (The notation (∧) stands for "acephalous"; thus, (∧) pher^d = ⏓ – ⏑ ⏑ – ⏑ ⏑ – –, i.e., a pher = ⏓ ⏓ – ⏑ ⏑ – –, without its first syllable, and expanded internally by a dactyl.) These two formulas with πείρατα, therefore, may be added to Nagy's list of cognate formulas, the partial glyconic from the Lesbian Lyric of Sappho 44 and the partial (∧) pher^d from Epic:[22]

Sappho	44.4	κλέος ἄφθιτον #
Epic	IX 413	κλέος ἄφθιτον ἔσται #
	44.3	τάχυς ἄγγελος #
	XVIII 2	τάχυς ἄγγελος ἦλθε #
	44.5	ἐλικώπιδα #
	I 98	ἐλικώπιδα κούρην #
	44.7	ἄλμυρον #
	iv 511	ἁλμυρὸν ὕδωρ #
	44.8	κἄμματα #

21Nagy 1974: 133.
22Nagy 1974: 121-122.

vi 111	εἵματα καλά #
vi 144	εἵματα δοίη #
vii 265	εἵματα ἕσσεν #
44.9	ἀθύρματα #
xviii 323	ἀθύρματα θυμῷ #
44.23	Ἴλιον #
IV 416	Ἴλιον ἱρήν #
44.31	προγενέστεραι #
ii 29	προγενέστεροί εἰσιν #
xxiv 160	προγενέστεροι ἦσαν #
II 155	προγενέστερος ἦεν #
Alkaios Z 21	ἀπὺ πειράτων #
Epic	ἐπὶ πείρατα γαίης #

Because these two formulas with πεῖραρ are formally equivalent to those from the Epics and Sappho 44, Nagy's explanation of the phraseological correspondence between the Epic hexameter and the Sapphic pentameter also accounts for ἀπὺ πειράτων # and ἐπὶ πείρατα γαίης #. Nagy argues that the Lyric phrases constitute not Epic imitation, but a "parallel inheritance of related formulas from related meters".[23] Sappho has not unconsciously inserted into her

[23]Nagy 1974: 134.

verses fragments of Epic formulas. If she had done so, Nagy contends, we would be "at a loss to explain the rigid correspondences of their placement in her meter and in Homeric hexameter".[24] In addition to the partial (∧) pher^{d} and glyconic formulas above, which occur at the end of the line, Nagy cites phraseological correspondences with the opening of hexameter lines for 16 out of 26 lines in Sappho 44.[25]

Alkaios' fragment and the Homeric hexameter provide a similar line-initial parallelism which occurs with the corresponding line-final πεῖραρ formulas. Besides the line-final cognates,

Lyric	Epic
ἀπὺ πειράτων #	ἐπὶ πείρατα γαίης #

a line-final + line-initial correspondence,

Lyric	Epic
ἀπὺ πειράτων #	ἐπὶ πείρατα γαίης #
# ἤλθες	# ἤλθομεν

is provided by xxiii 248-249:

ὦ γύναι, οὐ γάρ πω πάντων ἐπὶ πείρατ' ἀέθλων
ἤλθομεν.

[24]Nagy 1974: 125.
[25]See End-note J.

The metrically archaic Asclepiadeans of Alkaios Z 21 thus appear to contain a lexical pattern that is equally old: a partial glyconic phrase that is cognate with the partial (∧) pher[d] form of the same formula, used in the metrically innovative hexameter.

In view of these metrical indications that πείρατα γαίης is an ancient formula, it becomes significant that Alkaios' version of the phrase appears with Ὠκεάνω. Every time πείρατα γαίης denotes the ends of the earth in the Epics (and it does so in all but one instance of the phrase), the context includes the streams of Ocean. The juxtaposition of the two in Alkaios' verse indicates that not only the formula but also the contextual details in Homeric poetry are part of the Epic poet's inheritance of earlier lyric material.

These two instances of πεῖραρ in Alkaios' poetry show Aeolic Lyric to be a mixture of stylistic techniques both older and later than the Homeric Epics. The Lyric meters are older than the hexameter, and they can preserve formulas such as κλέος ἄφθιτον and ἀπὺ πειράτων that are the common inheritance of both lyric and epic poets. Comparison of such formulas with their counterparts in hexameter poetry can help us re-create the processes whereby epic poets adapted the old phraseology to the relatively new hexameter line.

On the other hand, the employers of these archaic metrical types, Sappho and Alkaios, are themselves generations later than the Epic bards. In addition to traditional songs, hymns, and stories, they also compose poems in these ancient rhythms not about the past but about the present, about people more human than heroic, about themselves and those they love and hate. They may allude to the Epic past to define the present, as does every Classical poet, but their choice of words in this "modern poetry" is motivated by a purpose and procedure different from that of the bard.

Bards are impersonal narrators of a long, basically familiar story. Line after line must flow from their lips. They must repeat or recombine or re-fashion by analogy phrases already fit for their metrical position, and, as the Homeric formulas reveal, masterful adherence to these technical restrictions generates, rather than impedes, the creation of rich figurative and conceptual meaning.

In their "new poetry" Sappho and Alkaios are different. They give their names, and those of their family, their friends, their enemies and their lovers.[26] They speak briefly, but they also play one of the roles in their

[26]For an enumeration of these names, see Page 1955: 130-139 for Sappho and 149-243, 295-297 for Alkaios.

poems, the role of themselves--and their part is in quotation marks. They too are limited by what their meter will allow. Indeed it is less flexible than the hexameter. But the bard's manipulation of traditional phraseology is inappropriate for this new poetic purpose. Poems about the politics and passions of specific historical moments permit less dependence on tradition. Although any poem is unique, it is uniquely true of individual lyric that it tries to tell what has never been told before or since. It is not necessary to say many things, many times, in many ways, but to say a single thing, once, and in the one appropriate way. Adherence to customary line-positions for words is not a help but a hindrance. The epic poet dances at length without rehearsal or choreographer, but in canonized movements. The lyric that is not merely personal, but individual, is the true improvisation. Each lyric embodies the moment.

D. SIXTH CENTURY ELEGY

Discovery of Mind and Mannerism: Poetry of Stylistic Transition

Solon

16 γνωμοσύνης δ' ἀφανὲς χαλεπώτατόν ἐστι νοῆσαι
μέτρον, ὃ δὴ πάντων πείρατα μοῦνον ἔχει.

Theognis

1172-1173 γνώμην Κύρνε θεοὶ θνητοῖσι διδοῦσι ἀρίστην
ἀνθρώποις· γνώμη πείρατα παντὸς ἔχει.

1077-1078 ὄρφνη γὰρ τέταται· πρὸ δὲ τοῦ μέλλοντος ἔσεσθαι
οὐ ξυνετὰ θνητοῖς πείρατ' ἀμηχανίης.

139-140 οὐδέ τῳ ἀνθρώπων παραγίνεται ὅσσ' ἐθέλῃσιν
ἴσχει γὰρ χαλεπῆς πείρατ' ἀμηχανίης.

Pigres μῆνιν ἄειδε, θεά, Πηληϊάδεω Ἀχιλῆος
Μοῦσα· σὺ γὰρ πάσης πείρατ' ἔχεις σοφίης.

Sixth Century Elegy is poetry of stylistic transition. Although the elegiac meter permitted the use of virtually any Homeric formula, Elegy is not formulaic. Adoption of whole phrases and adaptation of phrase-types from the Epics sometimes aids, but does not dominate, its composition. Solon and Theognis repeat phrases from Homeric poetry, but in fewer than one quarter of the extant lines: Solon - 47, about 21 per 100 lines; Theognis - 144, about 15 per 100 lines.[27] As for internal repetition, the same themes recur frequently both within and among the remaining collections. This is gnomic poetry and the vocabulary of these general truths seldom varies. But (to paraphrase Parry's definition of the formula) the same group of words is used in the

[27]Parry 1971: 280-281.

same metrical position to express a particular idea not regularly but occasionally, and then most often in the second half of the pentameter line, where the metrical rigidity (- ∪ ∪ - ∪ ∪ -, with no substitution allowed) would increase the need for "useful" phrases.[28] For the same reason, appropriation of Homeric word-patterns also occurs in the final pentameter segment, as the instances of πείρατα among these poems demonstrate.

The usage of πεῖραρ in Archaic Elegy exemplifies the genre's fusion of poetic properties. Only the plural occurs and only as the first word in the second pentameter segment. The shape of the phrase is an admixture of formulaic precedents. The joining of πείρατα with a genitive at the end of the line is paralleled by the Homeric occurrences of the word in the line-final Adonic segment:

πείρατ᾽ ἀμηχανίης ~ πείρατα γαίης, πείρατ᾽ ἀέθλων,
πείρατα τέχνης

The genitive + πείρατα + genitive collocation in

χαλεπῆς πείρατ᾽ ἀμηχανίης #

πάσης πείρατ᾽ ἔχεις σοφίης #

recalls the Homeric

ὑμῆς ἐπὶ πείρατα γαίης #

[28]Parry 1971: 281. See pp. 272, 274, for metrical usefulness as the defining distinction between "the real formula" and a phrase repeated for any other reason.

πολυφόρβου πείρατα γαίης #

πάντων ἐπὶ πείρατ' ἀέθλων #

and the Hesiodic μεγάλης ἐν πείρασι γαίης. The Epics, too, provide examples of πείρατα in collocation with παντός/ πάντων and ἔχειν:

πάντων πείρατα μοῦνον ἔχει ~ πάντων ἐπὶ πείρατ' ἀέθλων

πάσης πείρατ' ἔχεις σοφίης ~ νίκης πείρατ' ἔχονται

πείρατα παντὸς ἔχει

A hemiepes formula with πείρατα at its head appears first in the opening of two Hesiodic hexameters:

πείρασιν ἐν γαίης - υ υ - - -

πείρασιν ἐν μεγάλοις - υ υ - υ υ -

The latter of these shows the lack of spondaic substitution necessary for a second pentameter segment.

The meaning of πείρατα in early Elegy is also a Homeric inheritance. The Elegists have adopted the conceptual significance of the word established in Epic by the collocations πείρατα τέχνης and νίκης πείρατ' ἔχονται, where πείρατα assumes the force of "things which define or determine". This meaning of πείρατα offers an abstract expression ideally suited to gnomic meditations upon the function of such innovations in abstract language as γνώμη, occurring first in Theognis, γνωμοσύνη, used only by Solon in all Lyric, and ἀμηχανίη.

In fragment 16 Solon combines an inherited phrase-pattern and meaning of πείρατα with the novel γνωμοσύνη in order to express a point of view that differs from that of his predecessors. Maybe his debt to Epic also includes the choice of the central metaphor, τὸ μέτρον, and the decision to couple it with πείρατα, for the two notions are closely associated in xxiii 248-249:[29]

ὦ γύναι, οὐ γάρ πω πάντων ἐπὶ πείρατ᾽ ἀέθλων
ἤλθομεν, ἀλλ᾽ ἔτ᾽ ὄπισθεν ἀμέτρητος πόνος ἔσται.

Whether or not these lines contributed to the sequence of associations that created Solon's couplet, its teaching tactfully diverges from the Homeric world-view it recalls. In the words of Menelaos (VII 102) and Archilochos (111), personal courage was predicated on the belief that the line between victory and defeat was drawn by the hands of the gods (νίκης πείρατ᾽ ἔχονται ἐν ἀθανάτοισι θεοῖσι, νίκης ἐν θεοῖσι πείρατα). What Solon says is not an atheistic contradiction but rather a shift in focus from heaven to earth, from externalized, divine causality to internalized, human responsibility. In the pious and subtle silence of comparative allusion, he teaches those who can recall and compare that it is the μέτρον of human judgment alone that

[29]See pp.28-31.

controls the πείρατα not just of victory but of everything. Judgment is the sole ruler that can determine where all boundary lines are or ought to be. Upon the ability of the mortal mind to take this measure depends the rectitude of every edifice, not only the multiplying private shelters and the new marble temples of the archaic city-state, but particularly the political and moral structures fundamental to their support.[30] For this μέτρον, unlike a physical ruler, is invisible (ἀφανὲς). To see it is the most difficult thing (χαλεπώτατον), because it is perceivable only by the eye of the mind.

In a manner that parallels the difference between the emphases of Solon and those of the Epics, the placement of words in this couplet is only in part traditional. Besides the hemiepes with πείρατα as the first word, only the line-final νοῆσαι follows Homeric precedent. The remaining words either do not occur in the Epics or appear there in other positions. Solon has arranged them so as to underscore his meaning.

γνωμοσύνης δ' ἀφανὲς χαλεπώτατόν ἐστι νοῆσαι
  μέτρον, ὃ δὴ πάντων πείρατα μοῦνον ἔχει.

[30]For the foundations of a building as a metaphor for the morals that support justice, see Solon's description in 4.14f. of those Athenians who, because οὐδὲ φυλάσσονται σεμνὰ Δίκης θέμεθλα, provoke divine retribution in the form of slavery and revolution.

The abstract γνωμοσύνης, the most important word, comes first, but as a genitive whose subject, μέτρον, the fragment's crucial metaphor, is delayed by enjambment till the opening of the second line. There it receives added force by its parallel position with its genitive and the strong sense pause that follows it. The effect is grammatical suspense that ends in emphatic balance. Before the tension is relieved, however, it is increased by the juxtaposition of γνωμοσύνης and ἀφανὲς. The grammatical function of each word remains an uncertainty (matching the meaning of ἀφανὲς) until clarified by μέτρον. The complement of the hexameter creates another contrast between formal equipoise and semantic polarity: the rhythmic antiphony of 4- / 3- // 5- / 2- 3- syllable words is countered by the opposition between the meanings of ἀφανὲς and νοῆσαι, the two trisyllabic words that form the cadences of the line's two cola. The structural dynamics of the line thus reflect the couplet's meaning: the struggle that precedes the building of balance.

In the pentameter, the strong break after μέτρον is resisted by the chiastic order of grammatical relations and consonants in:

μέτρον, ὃ δὴ πάντων πείρατα μοῦνον ἔχει

a b b a

A B B A

The circular form pictures the general philosophical point: the interdependence of mental and physical measure. It also serves to highlight Solon's particular emphases: πάντων, by the stress between the metrical partition of the pentameter and the binding assonance of π's; and μοῦνον, by the grammatical and auditory recollection of μέτρον that unites end and beginning. The artistry is memorable.

Solon's couplet and 1172-1173 of Theognis display formal similarities that are difficult to account for with certainty.

γνώμην Κύρνε θεοὶ θνητοῖσι διδοῦσι ἀρίστην
  ἀνθρώποις· γνώμη πείρατα παντὸς ἔχει.

The position of γνώμην and the choice of the πείρατα hemiepes, complete with the double π's, mirrors Solon's verses. These parallels could reflect direct influence of one poet on the other, but in which direction, nothing intrinsic to the poems can determine.[31] It is also possible that the verbal structure as well as the general idea of these two couplets was part of the common, contemporary gnomic store.

The differences in the diction of these couplets, on the other hand, are more revealing. They point up the stylistic predilections that typify Theognis' verse. The

[31]See End-note K.

Megarian aristocrat appears to have taken particular delight in structural parallels and neatly patterned sounds for their own sake. Many of his couplets have the baroque quality of decorative variations, composed in cultivated leisure, upon current gnomic themes. In the center of 1172 the clever juxtaposition of opposite meanings and repeated θ's seems to have motivated the choice of not only the superfluous θνητοῖσι but also the somewhat bland θεοὶ διδοῦσι ἀνθρώποις. The arrangement may be Theognis' own. Neither θνητοῖσι nor διδοῦσι occurs in these positions in the Epics; θεοὶ precedes the caesura in hexameter poetry only once. Traditional placement is adopted when it promotes structural design, as with ἀρίστην, line-final in the Epics, and here completing a chiastic pattern of γνώμην θεοὶ θνητοῖσι ἀρίστην. The anaphora of γνώμη in the pentameter illustrates not only Theognis' penchant for homeoteleutic segments (γνώμη/ἔχει) but also the rhetorical underpinnings of his passionate and professorial tone. The point of the lesson, γνώμη, is repeated for Cyrnus; it heads a pithy summary, emphasized by asyndeton, of what Theognis goes on to explain in the remaining lines of the poem.

In 139-140 and 1077-1078 Theognis fits the abstract noun ἀμηχανίη (first in Alkman) into the traditional hemiepes of πείρατα + genitive in order to express the conceptual notion of human limitation.

οὐδέ τῳ ἀνθρώπων παραγίνεται ὅσσ' ἐθέλῃσιν
ἴσχει γὰρ χαλεπῆς πείρατ' ἀμηχανίης.

ὄρφνη γὰρ τέταται· πρὸ δὲ τοῦ μέλλοντος ἔσεσθαι
οὐ ξυνετὰ θνητοῖς πείρατ' ἀμηχανίης.

The phrase is grounded in the concrete usages of πείρατα in Homeric poetry as "bonds" and as "boundaries" between one land or world and another. The sphere of human possibility is limited by the πείρατ' ἀμηχανίης which constrain the extent of human knowledge of and power over the future, just as physical πείρατα bind Odysseus to the mast. Our mind and body are bound to the present by the πείρατα of mortality.

The enlargement of the phrase in 140 by a preceding adjective in the genitive, χαλεπῆς, seems to be an adaptation of an inherited pattern (see above, p. 134) to serve a formal tendency of Elegy, rhyming pentameter segments. Although it might appear from a continuous reading of the Theognidean corpus that this device is more characteristic of Theognis than of Elegy in general, the statistical frequency (by my count) of homeoteleutic hemiepes among Archaic elegists shows that Theognis is only typical.

Kallinos -	.2	(an insignificant figure, given the few lines that remain)
Tyrtaios -	.03	

Mimnermus -	.06
Xenophanes -	.13
Solon -	.07
Theognis -	.07

This circling of πείρατα with genitives appears, on the basis of Pigres' fragment, as a mark of the virtuoso elegist in general rather than Theognis in particular, for Artemisia's brother set himself the prodigious, but basically technical <u>tour de force</u> of inserting a pentameter after every line of the <u>Iliad</u>. The one vestige of his effort shows the customary coupling of πείρατα with an abstract noun, σοφία, in order to express conceptually the traditional role of the Muses (cf. II 484-493).

μῆνιν ἄειδε, θεά, Πηληϊάδεω Ἀχιλῆος
  Μοῦσα· σὺ γὰρ πάσης πείρατ' ἔχεις σοφίης.

To the extent that rhyming ends of the pentameter segments are, like the meter itself, a formal requirement of early Elegy (and the figures show they are by no means dominant), the genitive + πείρατα + genitive phrase may be termed formulaic, that is, a collocation for technical "usefulness". In 56 of the 103 instances of rhymed hemiepes in the Theognidean fragments, it is a noun + modifier combination that creates the antiphony. Both χαλεπός and ἀμηχανίη figure repeatedly in these formations:

78 χαλεπῇ / διχοστασίῃ

140 χαλεπῆς / ἀμηχανίης

180 χαλεπῆς / πενίης

182 χαλεπῇ / πενίῃ = 684 = 752

324 χαλεπῇ / διαβολίῃ

392 χαλεπὴν / ἀμηχανίην

638 χαλεποί / ἀμφότεροι

646 μεγάλῃ / ἀμηχανίῃ

1308 ἔργων / χαλεπῶν

Only once (588) is any form of χαλεπός placed in the pentameter other than at the end of the hemiepes. Since one of the two regular positions for χαλεπός in the Epics is before the penthemimeral caesura, i.e., at the end of the hemiepes, the placement of the word in order to achieve homeoteleutic segments seems to be another example of Theognis' transformation of Homeric usage into a stylistic adornment of the cultivated Elegy.

E. PINDAR

Champion of ἀρμονίαι

Pindar's three usages of πεῖραρ illustrate synoptically the poet's typical techniques and themes. Coming at the end of the Lyric Age, composed at the point when other Greek poets are transforming the Lyric into the Dramatic,

Pindar's odes, like the brief but radiant moments of victory they celebrate, represent the culmination of the discovery by Lyric poetry of humanism and abstraction. But just as the victors in the games were descended from heroes, so the Epinicia also embody a tradition with roots in the Epics. The lines of inheritance are visible in both the myths of the heroes around which the odes are framed and the Homeric diction that may be fitted into the dactylo-epitrite meter. The examples of πεῖραρ in Pindar exemplify not only this manipulation of Epic diction, but also the Lyric abstractions that accompanied the exploration during this period of moral and physical limits and the colonization of new-found space. Together, these instances of πεῖραρ show the poet to be, like the victors he praises, so completely in command of the contest's potentialities, so perfectly trained and exercised, that he can realize the full measure of the ἀρετή in his blood.

καὶ τάχα πείρατ᾽ ἀέθλων δείκνυεν πατρωΐων. <u>P</u>. 4.220

<u>Pythian</u> 4 is the most "Epic" of Pindar's Epinician odes. Jason's quest for the golden fleece dominates the poem. Instead of his usual practice of referring to the heroic past by brief allusions, Pindar narrates the story with a detailed leisure amounting to 193 lines. In the line above from this narration, Pindar proves his personal

control over his Epic inheritance. He has fashioned his "epyllion" not by simply repeating or re-combining Homeric phrases, but by free manipulation of traditional meanings and metrical patterns to serve his own poetic purpose.

In πείρατ᾽ ἀέθλων Pindar appears to have borrowed the Adonic formula in the words of Odysseus at xxiii 248:

ὦ γύναι, οὐ γάρ πω πάντων ἐπὶ πείρατ᾽ ἀέθλων.

The words sound the hexameter cadence, dividing Pindar's line so that the end of the phrase coincides with the end of the first metron, the hemiepes':- ᴗ ᴗ - ᴗ ᴗ - ⏑.[32] The Epic ring is deliberate and particularly emphatic, for the study by Jean Irigoin of Pindar's dactylo-epitrites demonstrates that coincidence of word-break and metron-break in them is quite rare. Pindar customarily employs word-bridge to suture the segments of his line.[33] It is the rhythm and tone alone, however, that Pindar has appropriated from the Homeric occurrence of this phrase.

The usage of πείρατ᾽ ἀέθλων carries Epic flavor, but no specifically allusive force. Pindar has repeated Odysseus' words, but not his meaning. The context of the phrase in the Odyssey makes it clear that πείρατ᾽ ἀέθλων is there a metaphorical application of the concrete meaning of

[32]For the notation and derivation of hemiepes:- ᴗ ᴗ - ᴗ ᴗ - and hemiepes':- ᴗ ᴗ - ᴗ ᴗ - ⏑, see Nagy 1974: 40.

[33]Irigoin: Paris, 1953: 30-31.

πείρατα γαίης: "the boundaries of the world of life and contests". In Pindar's line, on the other hand, πείρατα bears the conceptual sense established in such Homeric collocations as πείρατα τέχνης and πείρατα νίκης. What Medea points out to Jason are the "determinants" of the contests set by her father. The specifics of her revelation will be in Jason's hands like the goldsmith's tools: the means of effecting victory. Pindar does employ πείρατα in the metaphorical sense of the Homeric πείρατ' ἀέθλων, but in another place.

ἤτοι βροτῶν γε κέκριται
πεῖρας οὔ τι θανάτου. *O.* 2.30-31

This usage of πεῖραρ illustrates exactly how the word differs from τέλος. The τέλος θανάτου is the "performance" or "consummation" of death. Pindar's phrase is a metaphor, based like πείρατ' ἀέθλων, upon πείρατα γαίης/Ὠκεανοῖο:

Homeric
γαίης/Ὠκεανοῖο is to πείρατα
ἀέθλων (/θανάτου) is to πείρατα
as Pindaric
(ζωῆς/) θανάτου is to πεῖρας.

Again πεῖραρ means the line of demarcation between this world of life and the realm of death. But unlike the πείρατα γαίης, which can be seen, at least by heroes who can travel to the ends of the earth, the πεῖρας θανάτου is invisible. The force of οὔ τι κέκριται is that this boundary line has not been "set apart" so that it can be "discerned" and "judged" by mortals. Pindar's phrase pictures our ironically precarious position.

While within the ζωῆς πεῖρας, human life is a struggle to observe existing boundaries and to form new ones. To discern the πείρατα is to identify. We strive to know "our limitations", where we can go and what we can do in safety and success. To set the πείρατα is to create. Land becomes a farm or a stadium or an agora only after demarcation. The walls define the room, the house, the city. A society is shaped by its social and moral geography. People try to perceive, evaluate and fix limits in order to protect and promote their lives. For a while we succeed, at times gloriously.

Yet the end of every human life, that which defines it as a life and as human, is an inevitable boundary that cannot be foreseen. No detour can avoid it, but no sign can warn of its proximity. Our capacity to preserve and create life by discerning and drawing boundaries is itself so bounded that with any step we may cross the πεῖρας θανάτου. That "the πεῖρας θανάτου has not been distinguished" is precisely the πεῖρας of the human condition.

καιρὸν εἰ φθέγξαιο, πολλῶν πείρατα συντανύσαις
ἐν βραχεῖ, μείων ἕπεται μῶμος ἀνθρώπων· ἀπὸ γὰρ
κόρος ἀμβλύνει
αἰανὴς ταχείας ἐλπίδας. P. 1.81-83

The third usage of πεῖραρ by Pindar is part of a metaphor which, like the πεῖραρ ἔριδος in XIII 358, is a mystery. Again the results of our investigation into the etymology and usage of πεῖραρ supersede some explanations previously advanced and support another solution that, while not incontrovertible, satisfies the sense of the immediate and of the larger context. Again the interpretations vary according to what definition of πεῖραρ each commentator prefers and how a crucial verb is construed, in this case συντανύσαις, a hapax legomenon universally glossed as "stretch together".

Several scholars, beginning with the scholiast, have taken συντανύω as a synonym of συμπλέκτω, "to weave together, to intertwine". To those to whom πείρατα means "ropes", the metaphor is one of braiding or weaving. The scholiast says it is taken from nets.[34] The history of translations based on the image of plaiting include "twisting the strands of many things into a brief compass"

[34] ἡ δὲ μεταφορὰ ἀπὸ τῶν δικτύων.

(B. L. Gildersleeve, 1890),[35] "gathering together the loose ends of many matters in a single strand"(L. R. Farnell, 1932),[36] and "drawing narrow the strands of many matters" (R. Lattimore, 1947).

Others, who define πείρατα as "ends", propose a more abstract sense, almost beyond metaphorical force. Frequently Vergil's "sed summa sequar fastigia rerum" (Aen. 1.342) is cited, as by G. G. Cookesley in 1753 who translates: "contracting in a short space the principal points (literally, the extremities - highest points - heads)". E. Boeckh's Commentary of 1821 gives: "multarum rerum summam paucis complexus", and is followed in 1895 by E. Myers who renders: "comprehend in brief the ends of many matters". Pindar's recent translators, C. Ruck and W. Matheson, seem to adopt this tradition and to extend the phrase to a point of abstraction that, in mirroring contemporary idiom, eclipses all visual image:

> Were you, my art, to measure praise in due proportion, and yet
> succinctly in a word compress it all.

[35]Gildersleeve (1890: xliii) suggests that the image is from the creation of a rope-walk.

[36]Farnell 1932: 115. In his translation, however, he seems to describe not weaving so much as preparing tangled yarn for use: "in brief utterance straightening out a tangled skein".

The difficulty in taking πείρατα as "ends" in this context is not limited to the fact that Homeric usage of the word proves that it denotes not a point but a continuum. If πείρατα means "principal points", the verb, συντανύσαις, is, as Fennell observed, strangely anomalous and demanding of a tortuous interpretation.[37] If succinctness is the goal, why should one have to "stretch" the πείρατα together, if they are the "chief points"? How, in fact, does one "stretch" a "point"? Sequor does not equal συντανύω and the πείρατα are not fastigia.

Of the previous explanations of the phrase only the metaphor from weaving, with πείρατα rendered as "ropes" or "strands", is congruent with the sense of the verb.[38] This interpretation is consistent with a previous usage of πεῖραρ (i.e., as concrete "bonds") and provides an

[37]Fennell 1898: on P. 1.81-82: "'Having brought together by stretching' is the literal meaning of the word, but the process is not familiar except in archery. Now the drawing of a bow does not suggest comprehension, or compression, which we clearly want here. We must therefore consider συντανύω to have been formed as the correlative to ἐκτανύω and ἐκτείνω, the verbal element becoming quite subordinate to the preposition, and so seeming to acquire a sense opposite to its original meaning."

[38]For a variation upon this interpretation, a metaphor from spinning, see Bowra 1969: "Say enough and say no more, / And spin in slender twine / the threads of many tales . . . ." This rendering is perhaps the most satisfying of those based on πείρατα as "bonds" or "cords". It expresses the ideal of a καιρός-balance between πολλῶν and ἐν βραχεῖ.

image that could picture Pindar's poetic goal. Intertwining the strands of many things (πολλῶν) but in a short space (ἐν βραχεῖ) (i.e., with little space between the threads) would produce a fabric small in size but very closely-knit, apt adjectives for a style we often feel to be challengingly dense. There is Homeric precedent for the usage of τανύω in a description of weaving in XXIII 761.

A metaphor from weaving or braiding, while coherent and consistent with previous usage of the noun, is not, however, the only possible solution to the problematic phrase, nor does it accord particularly well with the structure and imagery of the immediate context and of the poem as a whole. A closely-knit fabric or a tightly-woven rope requires painstaking effort. Each is strong because it resists wear and tear. Each would be hard to untangle. What each fails to exemplify, however, is the notion of a difficult, delicate balance of opposites that we might reasonably look for in an appositive of καιρόν, the perfect moment--not too soon or too late, and the perfect amount--not too much or too little.

As if to make certain that the force of καιρόν would not be diffused, Pindar has ordered the quantitative terms upon which the sentence is built in accordance with the relationships they represent. The encircling of the participial phrase with πολλῶν and ἐν βραχεῖ portrays the harmonic tension that καιρόν implies.

καιρόν = πολλῶν ⇄ ἐν βραχεῖ

συντανύσαις

Compounding the dialectic is the interlocking alternation of expansion and contraction between πολλῶν and συν-, -τανυσαις and ἐν βραχεῖ. "Of many" looks forward to "having stretched" and "together" to "in a small space".

πολλῶν συν-τανύσαις ἐν βραχεῖ

a b a b

The phrase thus pictures both a three-part equilibrium and two interwoven doublets, both rest and movement at once.[39]

In juxtaposition with ἐν βραχεῖ comes the result of the achievement of perfect balance: μείων ἕπεται μῶμος, a second circle of adjective and noun, each dissyllabic and each beginning with μ. The two circles are stabilized by the sentence's heavy clausula, ἀνθρώπων. Next, the positive (καιρόν, πολλῶν ⇆ ἐν βραχεῖ, μείων μῶμος) is defined by the negative (κόρος). The graphic sense of the structure is thus:

καιρόν ⇄ πολλῶν ⇆ ἐν βραχεῖ ⇒ μείων - μῶμος vs. κόρος

πολλῶν συντανύσαις ἐν βραχεῖ

[39]See End-note L.

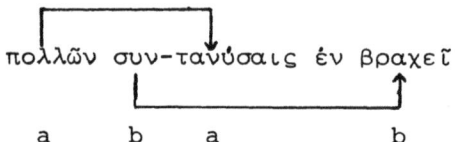

Society responds in sympathetic harmony (μείων - μῶμος) with the individual's difficult attainment of the καιρός.

The force of this pattern of meanings would seem to demand that πολλῶν πείρατα συντανύσαις ἐν βραχεῖ express an action whose end is the balance created by combining opposites in equal degree. In view of this clearly conscious structural artistry, "strands woven in a small compass" appears too pallid a picture. A new rendering of πείρατα is required that will yield an image more congruent with the eloquent outline of the phrase.

The usage of πείρατα in the Epic and Lyric offers two alternative translations, the concrete, "boundary lines", and the abstract, "determinants". The choice between them is suggested by the force of the verb, συντανύω. "To stretch so as to join together" is a precise, physical action, more appropriate to concrete "lines of demarcation" than to conceptualized "determinants". The verb does not so much invite the mind to think as the mind's eye to see. The phrase is more likely a metaphor than an abstraction--a metaphor for the attainment of the καιρός in speech, based upon the stretching and joining of boundary lines.

The meaning of the metaphor is qualified by πολλῶν and ἐν βραχεῖ. There are many πείρατα and only a little space. Most generally, the phrase means "having stretched out and connected the boundaries of many things but in a narrow interval of time and space". With πολλῶν and ἐν βραχεῖ the metaphor recalls Pindar's other expression of the καιρός as the epinician's aim.[40] To celebrate any victory, the poet must resolve the conflicting pressures of the many _laudanda_ and the brief time available, before surfeit (κόρος) elicits blame (μῶμος) from the people or the gods. The dilemma is stated explicitly in _P_. 8:[41]

> εἶμι δ' _ἄσχολος_ ἀναθέμεν
> _πᾶσαν_ _μακραγορίαν_
> λύρᾳ τε καὶ φθέγματι μαλθακῷ,
> μὴ _κόρος_ ἐλθὼν κνίσῃ
>
> 29-32

and at _N_. 10:

> _βραχύ_ μοι στόμα _πάντ'_ ἀναγή-
> σασθ', ὅσων Ἀργεῖον ἔχει τέμενος
> _μοῖραν_ ἐσλῶν· ἔστι δὲ καὶ _κόρος_ ἀνθρώ-
> πων βαρὺς ἀντάσαι.
>
> 19-20

The same synthesis of fullness and brevity is the general goal described overtly by πολλῶν and ἐν βραχεῖ and, more subtly, by -τανύσαις and συν- in the phrase above.

[40]For the καιρός as Pindar's poetic and moral goal, and analysis of the imagery related to it in various odes, see Lefkowitz 1963: 195-210.

[41]See also _P_. 9.76f., above n. 39.

The particular reference in this metaphorical appositive of the poetic καιρός emerges from closer consideration of the phrase as a whole and of its larger context in Pythian 1. The figure appears to be based upon demarcation. The one short phrase, like the καιρός it exemplifies, portrays a manifold process. Many πείρατα must be stretched, but not stretched only. They must also be connected. The object of the effort must be the delimitation of a whole with many integral parts. The whole itself must be subordinated to a strict temporal and spatial dimension (for ἐν βραχεῖ surely refers to both the space available for the many πείρατα and the time for stretching and joining). Indeed every word here expresses an aspect of measurement. Elsewhere the καιρός is associated in a general way with a μέτρον.[42] In the metaphor of Pythian 1, however, the multiplicity of the πείρατα, the vivid specificity of "to stretch so as to connect", and the subordination of the whole to restricted time and space evoke an image of the demarcation of an area both complex, elaborate and har-

42 δηρίομαι πολέσιν
περὶ πλήθει καλῶν· ὡς μὰν σαφές
οὐκ ἂν εἰδείην λέγειν ποντιᾶν ψάφων ἀριθμόν.
ἕπεται δ' ἐν ἑκάστῳ
μέτρον· νοῆσαι δὲ καιρὸς ἄριστος. O. 13.44-48

οὐκ ἐρίζων ἀντία τοῖς ἀγαθοῖς,
οὐδὲ μακύνων τέλος οὐδέν. ὁ γὰρ καιρὸς πρὸς ἀνθρώπων βραχὺ μέτρον ἔχει. P. 4.285-286

monious.

Both the immediate and the larger context--the ambiguous second-person verb, φθέγξαιο, the imagery of the lines that follow, and the ode's earlier emphasis on the founding of Aetna--all suggest that it is an ideally demarcated city-state to which the poetic καιρός is compared. Commentators have wondered whether φθέγξαιο refers to Pindar or to Hieron.[43] The question is raised by the almost imperceptible blending of second-person reference from apparently Pindar alone in καιρὸν εἰ φθέγξαιο, to either Pindar or Hieron or both in μὴ παρίει καλά (86), to apparently Hieron alone in νώμα δικαίῳ πηδαλίῳ στρατόν· ἀψευδεῖ δὲ πρὸς ἄκμονι χάλκευε γλῶσσαν (86). By recalling φθέγξαιο, γλῶσσαν links the honest use of speech urged in 86 with the verbal goal described above. In fact it is difficult to mark the point at which Pindar's focus shifts from the poetic to the political καιρός. The roles of poet and victor/ruler are further united as Pindar continues the second-person address, now overtly advice to Hieron. As Pindar's ideal was likened to the stretching and connect-

[43]For example, see Farnell 1932: on P.1.81: "Someone is here addressed in the second person, and again ll. 85-92, and it is natural to suppose they are the same person, namely the king, as ll. 85-92 obviously refer to him. But καιρὸν εἰ φθέγξαιο, etc., is certainly addressed to Pindar himself . . . ."

ing of <u>πολλῶν</u> πείρατα, so Hieron is the ταμίας <u>πολλῶν</u> who has <u>πολλοὶ</u> μάρτυρες πιστοί (88). The result of the proper government of the city-state is like that of the perfect composition of a poem: public opprobrium is minimized (εἴπερ τι φιλεῖς ἀκοὰν ἀδεῖαν αἰεὶ κλύειν, 90) by the avoidance of excess (μὴ κάμνε λίαν δαπάναις, 90; cf. κόρος ἀμβλύνει αἰανὴς ταχείας ἐλπίδας, 82-83)--but only minimized, for the μῶμος is only μείων, some φθόνος is inevitable (85), and "what the citizens hear (<u>ἀκοά</u>), especially about the merits of others, weighs heavily upon their secret spirit" (84). These formal and thematic links constitute a continuous chain between Pindar's address to himself and his comprehensive series (military, νώμα στρατόν; fiscal, ταμίας, μὴ κάμνε λίαν δαπάναις juridical, πολλοὶ μάρτυρες) of political directives to Hieron. This close connection between poet and patron suggests that the roles of the two inform each other and invites consideration of how Hieron's achievement might illuminate Pindar's metaphor of poetic excellence.

Pindar's description of his poetic καιρός as the extending and connecting of many πείρατα in a small area, and the blending of this picture with the sketch of ideal government by Hieron, together recall the previous references to Hieron's founding and ruling of Aetna. In 61-62 Pindar praises Hieron for founding (ἔκτισσε) the city θεοδμάτῳ σὺν ἐλευθερίᾳ Ὑλλίδος στάθμας...ἐν νόμοις; later in 70 he prays that Hieron might δᾶμον γεραίρων τράποι σύμφωνον ἐς ἡσυχίαν. Again verbal parallels fuse thematic links. The city's moral structure is "god-built freedom". Its laws rule like a chalk-line.[44] As Pindar is an architect of poetry, so metaphors of measuring and building describe Hieron's political creation. Reciprocally, the political goal of peace is likened to Pindar's ideally harmonious poem. The adjective, σύμφωνον, aptly qualifies the form and meaning of πολλῶν πείρατα συντανύσαις ἐν βραχεῖ. These reverberating cross-references combine to suggest that Pindar has likened the attainment of his poetic καιρός to the determination of a new city's spatial and moral geography. By so linking the poetic and political processes, the metaphor of 81-82 becomes an integral part of the imagery of the ode as a whole.

First, it recalls another metaphorical expression of Pindar's poetic aim earlier in the ode. The two images correspond like strophe and antistrophe. In the first image, too, a καιρός is the goal:

ἄνδρα δ' ἐγὼ κεῖνον

[44]See pp. 136-139 on Solon 16 and n. 31 for the description of moral and intellectual activity by a cluster of images that evoke land surveying, architecture and carpentry.

αἰνῆσαι μενοινῶν ἔλπομαι
μὴ χαλκοπάραον ἄκονθ' ὡσεί τ' ἀγῶνος βαλεῖν ἔξω παλάμᾳ δονέων,
μακρὰ δὲ ῥίψαις ἀμεύσασθ' ἀντίους. 42-45

Here, too, Pindar parallels himself with Hieron, as victor in the games. Here, too, the poet's success is portrayed in spatial terms and depends upon an ideal resolution of opposing forces. Pindar can become the victorious poet of praise only by hitting a point of harmonious balance, past the mark of his opponents, but within the set field of competition (ἀγῶνος). The alternative is the painful cacophony of defeat.

The javelin-metaphor links poet and victor not only because it alludes to the games, but also because it corresponds to the comparison between Hieron and Philoctetes in 50-57. As the poet must hit a καιρός-point with a javelin, so Hieron's victories in war (46-49) are likened to the mark attained by Philoctetes' arrow, that fatal weapon fated to be the sole instrument of peace. Philoctetes' arrow pierced the καιρός-point of victory by which the Trojan War and the cast-off's agony were balanced by the Greek peace and the hero's glory. By means of the mythic paradigm and its connection with the javelin-metaphor, Hieron's past victories, both Pythian and military, and Pindar's artistic aim are all paralleled. On the level of word-links, this cluster of analogous καιροί is joined with the poetic and political καιροί of 81-92 by the language of Pindar's prayer for Hieron's continued success. Pindar closes the allusion to Philoctetes with the hope that the god will be an ὀρθωτήρ to Hieron too, granting all he desires καιρόν (56-57). The adverb links the javelin-metaphor with its antistrophic counterpart.

Thus interrelated, both of Pindar's metaphors for his poetic ideal function in concert with the poem's integrating symbol: the golden harmony of the lyre and the bow.[45] Each recalls the ode's invocation to the χρυσέα φόρμιγξ of Apollo and the Muses, the instrument of a potential harmony with cosmic reverberations. When the strings are plucked at the proper intervals, and if everyone performs in perfect time to the lyre's rhythm, a song and a dance of peace pervade the divine and human spheres. A song of glorious praise, the harmony of the lyre, responds to the perfect bending of a bow, to the arrow precisely aimed at winning

[45]Burton (1962: 91) commends the "perfectly organized structure" of the ode and adds, "This impression of unity, clear enough even to us who can only read the poem, must have been much more vivid to those who heard it first performed, because the lyre of the opening verses, the symbol of music and what music stands for in this ode, was visible and audible throughout as the unifying instrument. This is indeed the only poem of Pindar which can be reasonably interpreted by the aid of symbolism, because the symbol itself, invoked at the beginning, can be seen and heard from first to last."

the contest or defeating the invader or founding a free and lawful city. Both poet and performers, victor and citizens have a role to play and a mark to hit--a καιρός to attain, and each καιρός answers the other in mirroring reciprocity.

Rendering πείρατα in 81 as "boundary lines" thus seems satisfactory at every level of consideration. It gives to πείρατα a meaning consistent with its etymology and inherited usage. With it, the phrase, πολλῶν πείρατα συντανύσαις ἐν βραχεῖ, acquires a sense both clear and wholly appropriate to the force of its own structure and to an appositive of καιρόν. The metaphor parallels the poet's goal of praising completely but briefly with the task of demarcating the ideal limits, both physical and moral, of a new city. The balance of spatial opposites that the image portrays recalls Pindar's earlier picture of poetic victory. The "harmony of the epinician lyre" is an aim like that of the competitor in the games who must stretch his arm (συντανύσαις), but to a limited extent (ἐν βραχεῖ) so that the javelin will connect with only the single point of καιρός.

Together the two metaphors perform the artistic function described figuratively in πολλῶν πείρατα συντανύσαις ἐν βραχεῖ, the function of delineating and conjoining the poem's several subjects. Because the javelin-image parallels the mythic paradigm of Philoctetes, and the metaphor with πείρατα recalls not only the javelin-image but also the founding of Aetna, the complex unity of all the _laudanda_, the Pythian prize, the military victories, and the new city, is achieved by retroactive reflection, ἐν βραχεῖ. Without the metaphor with πείρατα, the emphasis on Hieron as founder and law-giver and the elaborate injunction to ideal government would lie outside the ode's interradiating imagery. With the interpretation offered above, the figurative expression of Pindar's epinician καιρός adds another dimension to the harmonious attainments celebrated by the ode. Besides the victory in games and in war, "the harmony of the bow" is shown to include the defining of civil structures. As Pindar's poetic καιρός is identified with a κτίσις and a νίκη, so the bow and the lyre sound a single civilizing chord.

CONCLUSION

This study of the noun πεῖραρ illuminates the interdependence of formulaic artistry, the meaning of words in the Epics, and the connections between Homeric and Lyric poetry. In the Epics, the poetic properties of πεῖραρ are clear, and clearly due to strictly formulaic treatment of the word. Homeric usage embraces two concrete meanings, "boundary" and "bond", which, taken together, express a fundamental sense for πεῖραρ of "that which limits the outward extension of anything". The metrical characteristics of the plural, πείρατα, facilitate and sometimes promote poetically rich instances of these two concrete meanings, metaphors based upon them, and conceptualizations of the word's basic sense.

The metrical character of πείρατα, that is, combination with a noun or verb in an Adonic segment, is simple and strict, but it is by means of conformity with this metrical character that the poetic resources of the word are exploited and extended. The formulaic nature of πείρατα γαίης # is made to serve artistic ends. It is the only "word" in the Epic art-language for the "boundaries of the world". Any occurrence of the phrase, therefore, evokes this ultimate line of demarcation. When Odysseus uses the formula in his lie to Polyphemos, his words are rendered ironic. They remind us that, while Polyphemos' island is almost "the end of the world" for Odysseus, he is one of the heroes who returns from the πεῖρατα γαίης to tell the tale of the journey at Alkinoos' palace. Similarly, the frequency of πείρατα γαίης # as the "boundary lines between the land of life and the realm of death" makes possible the metaphor, πείρατ' ἀέθλων. The phrase is created by adherence to the metrical restrictions on the usage of πείρατα, in this case, by the analogical variation of the genitive complement. The same type of variation within the formal limits of the Adonic segment motivates the conceptualization of πείρατα evident in πείρατα τέχνης.

The coupling of πεῖρατα with a verb in an Adonic segment produces a wider range of poetic expressions. It permits the placement of the genitive complement before the noun, a sequence seen in a second metaphor based on πεῖρατα as "boundaries", ὀλέθρου πεῖραθ' ἵκηαι. Another metaphorical phrase, this one based upon the second concrete meaning of πείρατα, "bonds", is a composite of the phraseology and word-order in ὀλέθρου πείραθ' ἵκηαι and ἐκ δ' αὐτοῦ πείραθ' ἀνήφθω. A mid-verse version of this word-order is seen in the conceptual usage of νίκης πεῖρατ' ἔχονται.

The sum of the usages of πεῖρατα reveals both a basic

sense and a cluster of connotations that are activated by the three instances of the singular in the Epics. The use of a word as an apparently technical term for a settlement by a judge shows the grounding of the conceptualized "determination" in the concrete _terminus_. The πεῖραρ stretched by Zeus and Poseidon in an image of equally pitched battle is most likely a "bond", or cable in a tug-of-war, that bears the same attributes as the "boundary line" of battle for which it is a figure. This usage thus plays on both concrete meanings of the word. All meanings and associations of πεῖραρ are evoked by the πεῖραρ ὀϊζυός which bisects the world of Odysseus.

This survey of πεῖραρ in the Epics supports the premise that the formulaic process of composition is the means by which the poetic excellence of the Epics is achieved. In so doing, it also illustrates the ways in which the "grammar" of the art-language is constituted by metrical as well as syntactic rules, i.e., how meter affects the meaning of Homeric words. The semantic difficulties in the occurrences of πεῖραρ emerge, when examined in light of the formulaic method, not as inconsistencies indicative of a homonym, but as the products of a _Kunstsprache_ at work.

Comparison of the fundamental meaning of πεῖραρ with the Rigvedic usage of _párvan_ establishes that the two are semantic as well as morphological cognates. The Rigveda also conserves a synonym of *párvan* in *párus*. The lack of redundancy in the attested cases of these words suggests a suppletive declension, possibly prevented from paradigmatic leveling by the metrical usefulness of the forms preserved. The denotations of *párvan/párus*--"plant knot" possible once, "joint", the most frequent usage, and "point in time"--combine to reveal a fundamental sense of "that at which one things ends and another begins". This meaning of *párvan/párus*, together with the primary signification of πεῖραρ in the Epics, "that which limits the outward extension of anything", indicate an etymology: **per-u̯s/ u̯r̥/n̥*, "that which goes to the end", a deverbative from the goal-oriented sense of **per-*, "to go to the end-point, to go over to the other side".

The uses of πεῖραρ in Archaic poetry exemplify both pre-historical and historical connections between Epic and Lyric. The phrase ἀπὺ πειράτων # in a verse of Alkaios is the metrical cognate of κλέος ἄφθιτον # in Sappho 44, just as ἐπὶ πείρατα γαίης # is analogous to κλέος ἄφθιτον ἔσται # in Epic. The Alkaic and the Homeric phrases support the proposals of Nagy: the origin of the hexameter as a lyric verse-type, the use of what was once lyric phraseology to construct early epic lines, and the independent inheritance by Epic and Lyric poets of cognate formulas.

This example in the poetry of Alkaios of ancient phraseology requires us to revise our critical assumptions about the nature of Lesbian Lyric. The archaism indicates that Aeolic Lyric is not stylistically uniform. Not all forms that are like those in Epic constitute imitation of or allusion to the earlier poems. Some may reflect traditional lyric phraseology, inherited independently by Lesbian poets. Such usage is to be distinguished from the clearly conscious and ironic allusion to Epic evident in the second usage of πεῖραρ by Alkaios.

A combination of conservatism and innovation also characterizes the historical connections between Homeric and Archaic poetry. Dependence upon the meanings and formal patterns of the Epics is, naturally enough, most prominent in the Hesiodic poems, where the cosmographic function of πεῖραρ is elaborated, and a hemiepes formula constructed by utilizing the ν-movable is the only innovation. In later Lyric, as well, there are no alterations in the semantic range established in the Homeric poems, and the formal arrangement of the noun with a complement in the genitive occurs in every subsequent example. The continued vitality of the Epic usage of πεῖραρ reflects the more general traditional marks of the period: hexameter verse still typifies the pre-literate _Kunstsprache_, and all poetry is composed for oral performance.

The stylistic innovations of Lyric are allusion and increasing abstraction. In the adoption of νίκης πείρατα by Archilochos, we first encounter an evocation of earlier Epic usage. Such allusion can serve ironic and individual subjects, such as Alkaios' description of his brother's "heroic" feats as a mercenary. It can also, as in the lines of Solon, point up the differences between the Epic view of the gods as determinant of men's victories, and the vision in Sixth Century Elegy of the determining power and consequently the moral responsibility of the human mind. The expression of these new inward visions is made possible by combining πείρατα with new abstract nouns, such as γνωμοσύνη, from the growing conceptual vocabulary. Allusion as a stylistic option is made possible by the use of _litterae_, which transform a poem from "winged words" that live on only in memory to an object "more lasting than bronze," an identifying monument of its particular creator. As such, allusion is a mark of the movement from formulaic to literary art.

The manipulation of inherited meanings and formal patterns with πεῖραρ reaches a peak of versatility in the poetry of Pindar. The Epinician poet shows himself in the example from _Pythian_ 4 to be a master at "fitting together" a collocation, πείρατ' ἀέθλων, from one passage in the

Epics, with the conceptual meaning of πεῖραρ seen in another Homeric phrase, πείρατα τέχνης. In another usage, that of Olympian 2, he makes use of the metaphorical potential in πείρατα γαίης, but instead of combining with πείρατα some noun that refers to life in this world (γαίης), even a life of contests (ἀέθλων), he reinforces his emphasis on the irony of the human condition by completing the phrase with θανάτου. The etymology and usage of πεῖραρ in the Epics casts light on the difficult instance of πείρατα in Pythian 1. The background of the term excludes its interpretation as "end-points". The Homeric examples offer either "bond", "boundary" or "determinant". No choice can be proved, but a metaphor based on the stretching and joining of boundary lines harmonizes, in a manner typical of this "champion of ἁρμονίαι", with the formal artistry of the immediate context and the irradiating imagery of the poem's unifying symbol, the harmony of the lyre and the bow.

These illustrations of the stylistic developments of Archaic poetry, together with the illumination of meaning and formulaic artistry in the Epics, confirm the interrelationship of these aspects of early Greek poetry and the consequent need to approach them with an alliance of metrical, linguistic and poetic analysis.

APPENDIX A: R. B. Onians' Analysis of πεῖραρ in Early Greek Poetry

This monograph proposes a three-part method for determining the meaning of words in Epic: (1) contextual analysis of each instance of the word with no preconceived glosses in mind, (2) investigation of the degree to which the constraints of the formulaic method of composition affect the usage and semantic development of the word, and (3) comparison of the results of (1) and (2) with the Indo-European cognates of the word, if any exist. The insights and insufficiencies of the analysis of πεῖραρ in Homeric and Archaic poetry by Richard B. Onians in <u>The Origins of European Thought</u>, Cambridge, 1951, pp. 310-342, appear to be explainable in terms of the application or omission of these procedures.

Onians uses the most vexed instance of πεῖραρ in the Homeric poems as the starting point of his discussion, the πεῖραρ ἔριδος καὶ πτολέμοιο of XIII 358-360.[1] The context, he claims, demands that πεῖραρ mean some sort of concrete "bond" or "rope" and not an abstract "end" or "end-point".

[1]Cf. above, pp. 45-57.

His interpretation of the image as a whole, however, is perhaps not so congruent with the clear emphasis in the context upon a conflict between Zeus and Poseidon that mirrors the human hostility. Onians accepts the scholiastic explanation of ἐπαλλάξαντες as signifying "some manner of tying or fastening" (p. 311), and claims that the word "must here express the crossing over upon itself or tying of the rope to form a loop or open knot" (p. 318). In his conception, the two gods are "extending the loop or bond over both hosts, laying it on them both" (p. 319), so that the armies are bound together inextricably and the binding might be said to "loose the limbs of many." By forcing the gods to act together, as virtual allies against the men, this interpretation fails to accord with the sense of the lines which introduce the image:

> Two powerful sons of Kronos, hearts divided against each other,
> were wreaking bitter agonies on the fighting warriors,
> since Zeus willed the victory for the Trojans and Hektor ...
> while Poseidon emerging unseen from the grey salt water
> went among the Argives and stirred them, since he was angered
> that they were beaten by the Trojans and blamed Zeus

for it bitterly.

Indeed, the two were of one generation and a single father,

but Zeus was the elder born and knew more. Therefore Poseidon

shrank from openly defending them, but secretly

in a man's likeness was forever stirring them through the army.

(345-347, 351-357, trans. Lattimore)

The only alternative translation of ἐπαλλάξαντες that Onians considers is that mentioned and refuted by Leaf, "alternately" (p. 318). He insists that the later usages of ἐπαλλάσσω and its cognates (although he does not mention the earliest appearance of a cognate, ἐπαλλαγή, used by Herodotus of intermarriage), as well as the scholiastic interpretation, necessitate taking the participle as indicative of "making a knot". It is on this a priori ground that Onians eliminates the possibility of a metaphor based on a tug-of-war. He does not consider the simple "having crossed over". He implies that a tug-of-war can be pictured only if the participle is translated, "alternately".

However debatable any interpretation of the whole passage may be, Onians' claim that the context requires πεῖραρ = a concrete "bond" or "rope" seems incontrovertible. Similarly, his account of the πείρατα γαίης formulas is grounded upon the frequent collocation of the phrase with "the streams of Ocean". He concludes that πείρατα indicates not a series of end-points, but the earth's continuous boundary (pp. 315-317). Onians' explanation of this usage, however, seems prejudiced by an overriding interest in establishing a primary sense of πεῖραρ from which all other usages are derived, i.e., that the word originally designated not a function (e.g., "that which forms the outward extension of anything"), but solely a concrete object, "rope". From this original meaning, he argues, came the notion of a "bond" or "band" encircling the world.

Investigation of the Indo-European cognate of πεῖραρ, Rigvedic <u>párvan</u>, might have modified Onians' view. He does mention <u>párvan</u>, but accepts without question the customary glosses, "knot, joint, link", with "knot" as the primary sense. His conclusion is that "the sense of 'rope, knot, or bond' is clearly primitive as might have been expected. Efforts to derive noun or verb [πειραίνω] from an abstract notion of ending or limiting are futile" (p. 314). Onians does not seem to recognize the difficulties these three "primary senses" present for any etymology. Rather, it appears that because he wants πεῖραρ to mean a "binding rope" and because "rope" and "knot" are generally related terms, he is content to accept the given meanings for párvan without independent investigation. If he had surveyed the Rigvedic occurrences of the word, he would have found (if the conclusions of Chapter II are correct) only one possible instance of the meaning, "knot", and in that case, the knot of a plant: not a "bond", but a zoological "joint". Onians seeks to refute the contention that the original meaning of πεῖραρ was the abstract "issue" or "consummation" and to substitute the concrete, "rope" or "bond" as the primary sense. This goal appears to have dominated his evaluation of both the Greek and the Rigvedic evidence.

Having argued that the primary meaning of πεῖραρ is "rope" or "bond" and that the πείρατα γαίης formulas depend upon this sense, Onians turns to the collocations of ὀλέθρου πείρατα with ἐφάπτω. Here again, as with πεῖραρ ἔριδος καὶ πτολέμοιο, his translation of πείρατα as "binding ropes" accords well with the context. When ὀλέθρου πείρατα is combined with ἵκηαι, however, the force of the context is not so well respected. Onians claims that ὀλέθρου πείρατα is in each case not a "figure of speech", but "one of the images under which a whole people interpreted life and saw the workings of fate, the action of the gods in things human", an image like, for example, the Διός τάλαντα (pp. 325-326). The fate of men is conceived, he maintains, as "a bond fastened upon" them (pp. 326-327). While appropriate for the formulas with ἐφάπτω this interpretation does not suit the instances of ὀλέθρου πείραθ' ἵκηαι. The contexts of this phrase clearly indicate not the image of bonds fastened upon an individual, but a metaphor based upon the concrete meaning of πείρατα in the πείρατα γαίης formulas, the boundary line between one stretch of ground and another. By explaining πείρατα γαίης as an extension of πεῖραρ = "rope", Onians fails to include "boundary line" among the concrete senses of the word. By thus limiting the concrete range of the word, he is forced to take ὀλέθρου πείρατα as an image solely of ropes. Therefore, in order to establish that ὀλέθρου πείρατ' ἐφάπτω is an image of the bonds of fate, he must impose this picture upon ὀλέθρου πείραθ' ἵκηαι. In the process, the poetic flexibility of the ὀλέθρου πείρατα formula is submerged.

Another index of the difficulties caused by classifying πείρατα γαίης under πεῖραρ = "rope" is Onians' ambivalent interpretation of πείρατ' ἀέθλων as a type of ὀλέθρου πείρατα phrase. After maintaining that ὀλέθρου πείρατα always denotes the net-like "multiplicity of bonds" that is fate, he can say of πείρατ' ἀέθλων only: "Here too perhaps belongs οὐ γάρ πω πάντων ἐπὶ πείρατ' ἀέθλων / ἤλθομεν (Od. XXIII. 248f.) though the secondary meaning 'limits' might fit" (p. 322, n. 1). Examination of the context with no effort to limit πεῖραρ to a single concrete sense, suggests that πείρατ' ἀέθλων is a metaphor based upon the concrete meaning, "boundary line", in the πείρατα γαίης formulas.

When he proceeds to πεῖραρ ὀϊζύος, Onians again encounters a formula for which his translation of πεῖραρ as "bond" is contextually appropriate, although "rope-bond of fate" would be more fitting, if he is to preserve his notion of the common image of fate as constraining ropes and to avoid the question of why the metrically equivalent δεσμόν is not used here for simply a "bond". What is precluded by the predetermination of πεῖραρ as "rope-bond" is an appreciation of the added connotation of "boundary line of sorrow", lent to πεῖραρ ὀϊζύος by the meaning of the word in the πείρατα γαίης formulas and activated by the context.

In accordance with his account of πεῖραρ ὀϊζύος and of πείρατα ὀλέθρου, γαίης, and ἔριδος, Onians takes the occurrence of νίκης πείρατα in VII 102 and Archilochos 111 as another version of the "rope-bonds of fate". By itself, this interpretation is perhaps open to debate or amplification, but it is not impossible. The argument he builds upon the rest of the phrase is, however, unsound. Because the formula is coupled with ἐν θεοῖσι, Onians claims, "What lies 'upon the knees of the gods' is the fate the gods spin (θεοὶ ἐπέκλωσαν). πείρατα should, we might now suspect, be related to spinning" (p. 334). He further reasons that because such words as ὀλέθρος and ὀϊζύς are both genitive complements of πείρατα and objects of θεοὶ ἐπέκλωσαν, πείρατα must mean "the products of spinning, i.e., thread" (pp. 334-335).

In support of this extension of πεῖραρ = "rope" to πεῖραρ = "thread", Onians adduces the problematic occurrence of πείρατα in Pindar, _P_. 1.81. His reasoning here is circular. He claims the usage proves that πεῖραρ could mean "woof-thread", notes Gildersleeve's remark, "A homely figure seems to underlie πείρατα συντανύσαις," and then concludes that "...perfect sense is given if πείρατα means woof-threads," and "weaving is just such a 'homely figure' as is recognised as necessary" (pp. 338-339). A metaphor from weaving is possible here. In Epic the verb τανύω is used of weaving (XXIII 761, not cited by Onians). Such a metaphor is not, however, proved by Onians' argument. Even supported by the Homeric usage of τανύω, this reading of the metaphor may be challenged on the basis of contextual fitness.

Having limited himself to a primary significance of πεῖραρ as concrete "rope", "bond" or "thread", Onians declares that the three remaining usages of πεῖραρ in Epic "scarcely allow precise interpretation" (p. 341): the πεῖραρ obtained from the "umpire" in the Shield's City of Peace, XVIII 501; the ἑκάστου πείρατα that Nestor tells his son before the chariot race, XXIII 350; and the goldsmith's tools, the πείρατα τέχνης, iii 433. In order to give a sensible translation of each, Onians must stretch his "original meaning" beyond its semantic limits by juxtaposing it with the sense the context requires. Of the first he says: "The idea may be of a bond, a binding decision, a fastening or closing of the dispute." Of the second (with which he properly classes the πείρατ' ἀέθλων given by Medea to Jason in P. 4.220): "Here something like 'strands' or fastenings' might suffice, means by which each feat had been fastened, constructed, or might be traversed or accomplished." Of the third (reading ὅπλα as "cord" or "ship's tackle"): "...'fasteners of his craft' would harmonize with the then current method of making joints or fasteners in metal work by bonds, δεσμοί" (p. 341). Since Onians nowhere takes account of the formulaic method of composition, it cannot help him explain these semantic developments of πεῖραρ. Of the interpretations of these passages offered in this study, that of πείρατα τέχνης is most aided by considerations of how the style might have motivated the development in diction from the concrete to the conceptual sense of πείρατα, the sense of the word favored by the Sixth Century Elegists.

APPENDIX B: Metrical Distribution of *párvan* and *párus* in the Rigveda

Simple Forms

Exception:

Ab. singular - only the form of *párvan* occurs, *párvaṇo*

Triṣṭubh: 1 2 3 4 5, 6 7 8 9 10 11

υ υ - (10.68.9d)

pár-va-ṇo (C)

vs. *páruṣas* which *would* satisfy the statistically most frequent pattern and better than *párvaṇo*: - υ - vs. *páruṣas* υ υ -

exception?

Instr. singular - only the form of *párus* occurs, *páruṣā*

Gāyatrī: 1 2 3 4 5 6 7 8 (9.15.6b)

x x x x

pá-ru- ṣā

vs. *párvaṇā*, which would also fit

exception?

Instr. plural - only the form of *párvan* occurs, *párvabhir*

Triṣṭubh: 1 2 3 4, 5 6 7 8 9 10 11

υ υ - (10.79.7d)

pár-va-bhir (C), the second most frequent pattern - υ -

vs. párurbhir, which would give a short syllable to slot 5, but a long syllable to slot 6, a pattern which very seldom occurs (Atkins 1968: 683)

NA singular - only the form of párus occurs, párus/r

Jagatī: 1 2 3 4 5 6 7 8 9 10 11 12

υ - υ x

(10.100.5a) pá-rur

vs. párva, which would give a long syllable to slot 9

G singular - only the form of párus occurs, páruṣaṣ

Triṣṭubh: 1 2 3 4 5, 6 7 8 9 10 11

υ υ -

pá-ru-ṣaṣ (C) (10.53.1)

vs. párvanas which would give a long syllable to 6; in this position υ υ - is seventeen times more frequent than - υ - (Atkins 1968: 683)

Loc. singular - only the form of párus occurs, páruṣi

Jagatī: 1 2 3 4, 5 6 7 8 9 10 11 12

υ υ – (7.50.2a)

pá-ru- ṣi, the third most frequent pattern, υ υ υ (Atkins 1968: 683)

vs. párvaṇi which would give a long syllable to slot 5, the very infrequent – υ υ

OR

párvan which would not provide three syllables

Loc. plural - only the form of párvan occurs, párvasu

Jagatī: 1 2 3 4 5 6 7 8 9 10 11 12

– υ x

(8.48.5b) pár- va-su

vs. páruṣṣu which would give a short syllable to slot 10 and a long syllable to slot 11

NA plural - only the forms of párvan occur, párvāṇi and párva

Triṣṭubh: 1 2 3 4 5 6 7 8 9 10 11

x – x –,

(1) pár-vā- ṇi (10.87.5b)

x – x,

(2) pár- vā- ṇi (4.22.2d)

	- x,	- x
(3)	pár- va (C)	pár- va
	(1.61.12c)	(4.19.9d)
	pár- va (C)	pár- va
	(10.89.8b)	(7.103.5c)

vs. párūṃsi which would
in (1) give a short syllable to slot 2
in (3) exceed the number of available slots

exception?
in (2) fit as well as párvāṇi

Āmreḍita-Compounds

Instr. singular - only the form of párvan occurs, párvaṇā-parvaṇā

Jagatī:	1	2	3	4,	5	6	7	8	9	10	11	12	
					ᴗ	ᴗ	-	-	ᴗ	-			(1.94.4)

pár-va- ṇā- par- va- ṇā, showing
the very acceptable, - ᴗ - / - ᴗ -

vs. páruṣā-paruṣā, which would give a short
syllable for slot 8, the highly irregular
ᴗ ᴗ - / ᴗ ᴗ - (Atkins 1968: 683)

NA singular - only the form of párus occurs, párus-paruḥ/h

Triṣṭubh:	1	2	3	4,	5	6	7	8	9	10	11
	x	-	x	-	ᴗ		ᴗ				

pá-rus-pa- rur (V) (1.162.18d)

vs. *párva-parva*, which would give a short syllable to slot 2

Anuṣṭubh:	1	2	3	4	5	6	7	8
					ᴗ	-	ᴗ	x

pá-rus-pa- ruḥ (10.97.12b)

vs. *párva-parva*, which would give an inappropriate trochaic cadence

Loc. singular - only the form of *párvan* occurs, *párvaṇi-parvaṇi*

Anuṣṭubh:	1	2	3	4	5	6	7	8
			x	x		-		x

pár-va- ṇi-par-va- ṇi (10.163.6)

vs. *páruṣi-paruṣi*, which would give an irregular short syllable to slot 6

END-NOTES

A (Introduction, footnote 7). Parry (1971: lxii) notes the rarity of criticism which attempts "to grasp both the existence and the poetic effect of the formula, and then to show how it becomes part of an artistic construct". A superb example of this rare criticism is the new book of Nagler (1974), which pursues in its treatment of groups of related phrases and narrative motifs, the over-all aims of Chapter I of this monograph. Nagler's study does not address our semantic problems with the Epics, but his methods and results will greatly aid others with that goal. Another recent study designed to dispel the notion of an intrinsic opposition between formulaic technique and aesthetic excellence is Patzer 1972. The range of this book, like that of Nagler's, is wide, including formulas, typical scenes and basic narrative patterns. Nagler's work is unique, however, in its ability to sophisticate our appreciation of the poetics of formulaic art. Nagler succeeds in portraying the art-language "in motion"; we are led by his demonstrations to perceive the Kunstsprache as a process rather than a static entity, to understand the "formula" as a "verb" rather than a "noun".

For exemplary studies of artful characterization by means of formulaic diction, see A. Parry 1956 and 1966, Donlan 1971, and Segal 1971a.

B (Introduction, footnote 12). On the vanity of trying to prove the poetic value of formulaic style in the usage of one word, cf. A. Parry 1971: lv: "The negative case for any criticism of Homer dealing with the single word has been well put in the thoughtful article of F. M. Combellack, 'Milman Parry and Homeric Artistry.' Combellack concludes: 'For all that any critic of Homer can show, the occasional highly appropriate word may, like the occasional highly inappropriate one, be purely coincidental--part of the law of averages, if you like, in the use of formulary style." In contrast to this contention, Nagler (1967) has shown the poetic power and versatility of κρήδεμνον to be a function of its formulaic treatment. In addition, the analyses of one category of single words, epithets, of Pope (1960) and Whallon (1969) illuminate the aesthetic virtues in the deployment of these words in the

Epics. Most similar in procedure to this monograph is the study of A. A. Parry (1974) in which each instance of the single epithet ἀμύνων is analyzed, with full attention to its metrical characteristics, in order to establish its etymology and elucidate its poetic effects in the Epics.

C (Chapter I, footnote 9). Björck (1937-1938: 148) glosses πείρατα τέχνης as "la limite suprême de l'habileté". Yet it is difficult to see exactly what he has in mind. The tools can only be "that which perfects" or "that which puts the ultimate boundary upon" the τέχνη, whether τέχνη means "the art" or "the work of art". One might conclude that Björck understood "la limite suprême de l'habileté" in this way, except for the fact that he objects to interpreting πείρατα as "accomplishers", as do Merry and Riddell 1886: s.v. xii 51. Björck claims that this gloss requires an unparalleled change in point of view.

Björck illustrates his reading of πείρατα as "perfection" or "the phenomenon representing the highest degree" by the usage of πέρας in:

(1) ὅταν ἤ τὰ πράγματα λάβῃ τέλος καὶ μηκέτι δέῃ βουλεύεσθαι περὶ αὐτῶν ἢ τὸν λόγον ἴδῃ τις ἔχοντα πέρας ὥστε μηδεμίαν λελεῖφθαι τοῖς ἄλλοις ὑπερβολήν.

Isoc. Panegyricus, 5

(2) τῆς τέχνης πέρας τοῦτ᾽ ἔστιν.

Posidippus, com. fr. 26.17 Kock

(3) Μάρκος Ἀπίκιος Ῥωμαῖος (the famous gourmand) ὡς ἦν ἀσωτίας πέρας, οὐδεὶς ἀντιφήσει.

Aelian, fr. 111, Hercher

The Homeric phrase, however, is an appositive of ὅπλα, and the tools cannot be the "perfection" of the τέχνη in the same way that Marcus Apicius was the πέρας of ἀσωτία. In Posidippus' phrase, if πέρας means the "perfection", the τοῦτ᾽ was not a tool. The product of the tools, like the λόγος, might be able ἔχειν πέρας, but not the tools themselves.

D (Chapter I, footnote 13). The singular, πεῖραρ, is used at XVIII 501 in the same abstract sense of "determination" to denote a legal judgment: ἄμφω δ᾽ ἱέσθην ἐπὶ ἴστορι πεῖραρ ἑλέσθαι. This usage, too, appears to be a conceptual extension of the concrete significance of πεῖραρ as "line of demarcation" between two opposing realms (see pp. 43-45). Comparison between this verse from the description of Achilles' shield and νίκης πείρατ' ἔχονται suggests the possibility of a juridical reference in Menelaos' words. What Menelaos may be saying is: "the gods are the judges of men's battle trials."

Compare the later legal idioms, πέρας ἔχειν and πέρας λαμβάνειν, in

ἑστ' ἂν τὰ πρὸς αὐτὸν ζητούμενα πέρας λάβῃ

and

ἐνθάδε δύναται τὸ πράγμα πέρας ἔχειν

(Grundzüge und Chrestomathie der Papyruskunde, L. Mitteis and U. Wilcken, Band II, 1912, 54.11 and 87.12). Björck (1937-1938: 144) cites these passages in evidence that πέρας in these idioms means "the final decision between two opposites", an apt paraphrase of the conceptual force latent in the concrete.

For the usage of the plural in a juridical sense, dependent upon the concrete function of πείρατα, see A. R. IV. 1201-1202 (the subject-judge is Alkinoos):

αὐτὰρ ὅγ' ὡς τὰ πρῶτα δίκης ἀνὰ πείρατ' ἔειπεν
ἰθείης,

On the other hand, Menelaos' usage of πείρατα may bear only the general force of "determination" and may thus be parallel to the verse that probably served as model for Apollonius' line, namely XXIII 350 (Nestor is the speaker):

ἕζετ', ἐπεὶ ᾧ παιδὶ ἑκάστου πείρατ' ἔειπε.

On this verse see further pp. 41-43.

E (Chapter I, footnote 18). The supposition that all instances of πεῖραρ are categories of the general meaning, "end", requires Björck (1937-1938) to argue that if ὀλέθρου πείρατα means "the end that is destruction" when combined with ἵκηαι, the sense must be the same where ἐφάπτω is the verb. He cites Τρώεσσι δὲ κήδε' ἐφῆπται (II 15) and the Attic idiom, αἰσχύνην περιάπτειν τινί, in support of his claim that ἐφάπτω does not imply the use of ropes. This much is surely correct. These parallel phrases do not, however, prove that πείρατα here is an abstraction equaling τέλος. A verb meaning "to fasten upon" does not imply any particular sort of bonds like "ropes", but it does mean that the phrase is a metaphor, based upon binding. With ἐφάπτω, the phrase would be figurative, even if the object were τέλος or κήδεα.

The collocation of κήδεα and ἐφάπτω in II 15 is another metaphor, cognate with phrases like ἐκ δ' αὐτοῦ πείρατ' ἀνήφθω. It is a semantic correlative of ὀλέθρου πείρατ' ἐφῆπται that permits the placement of an object like Τρώεσσι in the second half of the verse, since it confines the metaphor to the Adonic segment:

Ἥρη λισσομένη, Τρώεσσι δὲ κήδε' ἐφῆπται II 15
vs.
ὡς ἤδη Τρώεσσι ὀλέθρου πείρατ' ἐφῆπται VII 402

F (Chapter I, footnote 22). The fact that these two instances of πείρατα reflect two semantic applications of one and the same word sheds light upon the problem of the apparently diverse usages of the verb derived from πεῖραρ, πειραίνω/περαίνω. The Homeric lines in question are:

(1) ταῦτα μὲν οὕτω πάντα πεπείρανται, σὺ δ' ἄκουσον
xii 37
σειρὴν δὲ πλεκτὴν ἐξ αὐτοῦ πειρήναντε
xxii 175=192
πῆξε δ' ἄρ' ἐν μέτροισι ταμὼν δόνακος καλάμοιο
πειρήνας διὰ νῶτα διὰ ῥινοῖο χελώνης.
h. Merc. 47-48

According to Chantraine 1963: I 421, 433, two different verbs lie behind πεπείρανται and πειρήναντε/πειρήνας. Interpreting πεπείρανται as a perfect middle with the same vocalism as the present and citing πειρήναντε as an example of an aorist with no attested present, Chantraine implies the existence of two separate verbs, the first meaning something like "fulfill" or "accomplish" and the second, "bind" or "fasten". On the basis of this survey of πείρατα in Epic, however, it seems possible to define a basic sense of πειραίνω, analogous to that of πείρατα, from which these two derivational meanings might stem. If the primary meaning of πειραίνω is "to form the limit of the outward extension of anything", the verb might easily take on a conceptual ("to define or determine") and a concrete, causative ("to make something function as a binding") signification, comparable to the meanings of πείρατα itself.

πεπείρανται, "it is defined or determined"

IS TO

πείρατα, "determinants"

as in, e.g., ἕζετ', ἐπεὶ ᾧ παιδὶ ἑκάστου πείρατ' ἔειπε

AS

<u>πειρήναντε</u>/<u>πειρήνας</u>, "having made X function as a binding"

IS TO

<u>πείρατα</u>, "bonds"

as in, e.g., οὐδ' ἔτι δεσμά σ' ἔρυκε, λύοντο δὲ πείρατα πάντα

There seems as little need to postulate a homonym in the case of πειραίνω as in that of πείρατα.

<u>G</u> (Chapter I, footnote 25). Aristarchus is credited with the assumption of two πεῖραρ's, one of strife and one of war, in Scholia A on 359. Scholia A on 358 paraphrases: "For the τέλος is expressed figuratively as the extremities on each side interwoven, one of the Trojans and one of the Greeks . . ."; Scholia B on 358 adds: ". . . just as those who make strong bonds by casting τὰ πείρατα of them upon other bonds and weaving them together thus form a bond that is hard to break, so also the gods wove the φιλονικία of the armies so that it became δυσδιάλυτον . . . . For he named the πέρας of strife and the πέρας of battle as if (they were) τὰ πείρατα of ropes." The inconsistency between this interpretation of the passage and the adjectives of 360 is noticed by Ameis 1879: on 345-360.

The modern versions of the scholiastic tradition include Arnold 1852: "having interlaced the ends of the fight, they stretched them indissolubly on both sides." Munro (1847) first claims that "the battle is like a piece of rope (πεῖραρ) passed over both by the gods (ἐπαλ.) and drawn tight (ταν.) by which accordingly they knit together inseparably . . . " and then says there is a play between the literal sense of "the end of a rope" and the abstract idea of "the ends of destruction" seen in ὀλέθρου πείρατα. The commentary of Leaf and Bayfield (1936) displays a similar confusion: "'they twain with changing fortune (ἐπαλλάξαντες) for both sides stretched (ἐπὶ with τάνυσσαν) the rope of stubborn conflict and levelling war.' The method of expression is difficult, but the general sense is clear: the two gods keep the tide of victory swaying backwards and forwards by alternately pulling each army with <u>ropes</u>." (My emphasis.)

H (Chapter I, footnote 26). Besides this collocation with πεῖραρ, τάνυω/τείνω is used of (1) stretching out flexible objects: an animal on a spit, a human body on the ground (sometimes with ἐπὶ γαίῃ/χθονὶ) or in the air (Melanthios hanging from the rafters), a chin strap, straps around the chest, a bow string, reins either "from the chariot rail" or "backwards", a thong, a string of the lyre, the jaws, a rainbow, a hurricane (λαῖλαψ), the night (ἐπὶ βροτοῖσι); and metaphorically, ἔρις, κάκος πόνος (ἐπὶ Patroklos), κρατερὴ ὑσμινὴ (ἐπὶ Patroklos), πολεμός (ἐπὶ σφίν) and (2) laying out inflexible objects: the props under ships, a sword under the waist, the spits above a bed of coals, a spear upon (ἐπὶ) the deck of a ship. From the stretching action required in order to stretch out something like a bow string or the ships' props, the verb acquires the meaning "to pull", along the floor. The verb τανύω is used in this sense in the middle of horses and mules who "stretch themselves" or "pull" (τανύοντο) and at II 324 with the objects pulled, the reins, in the dative, and with the new direct object, the team of horses, only implied: ὅπως τὸ πρῶτον τανύσῃ βοέοισιν ἱμᾶσιν. Similar is the use at XVI 475 of the passive τανύσθεν with horses as the subject and the reins in the dative. From this elliptical usage comes the meaning, "direct or steer toward" as in Pindar, Paean, IX 49.

The use of the perfect τέτατο with δρόμος at XXIII 758 and viii 121, "the race course was stretched from the starting place", makes it appear that the course was marked by stretching out something on the ground to form its boundaries. These two lines refer to the moment before the race begins. By an inversion of subject and object parallel to that in "the horses were pulled by the reins", the end of the race is described in XXIII 375 by the phrase: ἵπποισι τάθη δρόμος, "the course-length was stretched by the horses". Compare the English, "the home stretch".

If the δρόμος was marked by stretching out something to form its boundaries, it is possible that the demarcations were called the πείρατα. With this connotation the use of πείρατα (XXIII) to describe Nestor's directions to Antilochos before the horse race would become a sort of pun: the father explained not only the "determinants" but also the "boundary lines" of the race. Such a double entendre would be appropriate in view of Antilochos' subsequent skill in using a narrow passage in the track to force Menelaos to let him pass.

I (Chapter I, footnote 31). Ernest (1824) glosses ἐπαλλάσσω as "in utramque partem trahere". Brandreth

(1841) translates: "terminum alternantes, super ambos tetenderunt". Duntzer (1866) reads the participle as "wechselnd, in dem bald der eine bald andere eintrat". According to LSJ a tug-of-war is the image and the verb means "pulling alternately this way and that" only if the variant ἀλλήλοισι (found in one of the two editions of Aristarchus used by the scholiasts) is accepted.

Others have interpreted the image as a tug-of-war without commenting upon ἐπαλλάξαντες. Among them are Doederlein (1863), Trollope (1827), Heyne (1832), and Van Leeuwen (1913). In their note on xii 51 Merry and Riddell (1886) conclude that the adjectives, ἄρρηκτόν τ' ἄλυτόν τε, and the verb, τανύω, make it certain that the metaphor is of a tug-of-war, but then insist that πεῖραρ was used as a technical term for the "rope-end" away from the speaker, a usage parallel to that of ἀρχή, for the "rope-end" nearest to hand. They then conclude that "the gods are dragging at the ends of a rope" and that πείρατα must have become a familiar word for "ropes". This is another version of the "indissoluble end" inconsistency.

J (Chapter III, footnote 25). Nagy 1974: 126-128:

44.1	# Κυπρο
iv 83	# Κύπρον
44.2	# κάρυξ
viii 62=471	# κῆρυξ
44.3	#῎Ιδαιος
V 20, VII 416	#᾿Ιδαῖος
44.5	#῞Εκτωρ
III 116, etc.	#῞Εκτωρ
44.6	# Θήβας
h. Ap. 228	# Θήβης
44.8	# πόντον
VII 6, etc.	# πόντον
44.9	# πορφύρα
iv 298, etc.	# πορφύρε'
x 353	# πορφύρεα
44.10	# ἀργύρα
XXIII 741, etc.	# ἀργύρεον

44.12	# φάμα
xix 100, 105	# φήμην
44.13	# αὖτικ'
I 386, etc.	# αὐτίκ'
i 324, etc.	# αὐτίκα
44.14	# ἆγον
vii 324, xx 277	# ἦγον
44.16	# χῶρις δ' αὖ
iv 130	# χῶρις δ' αὖθ'
XXIV 278	# χῶρις δ' αὖτε
44.17	# ἵπποις
III 260, etc.	# ἵππους
44.24	# αὖλος
xviii 495	# αὐλοὶ
44.26	# ἄειδον
xvii 519, etc.	# ἀείδῃ
44.27	# ἆχω θεσπεσία
viii 159, etc.	# ἠχῇ θεσπεσίῃ
44.28	# πάντᾳ
I 384, etc.	# πάντῃ
44.29	# κράτηρες
VI 528	# κρητῆρα

K (Chapter III, footnote 31). The customary chronology of early Greek Elegy has recently been challenged by West (1974), who places the beginning of Theognis' political and poetic career in the last half of the seventh, rather than in the sixth century. Along with this new dating, he offers a revision of our general assumptions about literary relations between Solon and Theognis: "Solon's poems are closer to Theognis' in content and language than anything else we have. This is partly because similar events were afoot in both cities, but there is a case for direct influence of one poet on the other. It has always been taken for granted that Theognis imitated Solon (who is certainly the more imaginative and forceful writer), but for no other reason than that he has been dated later than Solon. The reverse relationship is equally possible" (West, p. 70). It is quite true that nothing within these couplets can tell us which was composed first. Only the mutual affinities and the differences between them are certain.

L (Chapter III, footnote 39). For a similar but less elaborate structural analogue of the καιρός, see *P.* 9.76f.:

A

ἀρεταὶ δ' αἰεὶ μεγάλαι πολύμυθοι
βαιὰ δ' ἐν μακαροῖσι ποικίλλειν

B A a b

ἀκοὰ σοφοῖς· ὁ δὲ καιρὸς ὁμοίως
παντὸς ἔχει κορυφάν.

b a

The pattern of interlocking doublets is paralleled in *N.* 1. 18, although the tension between καιρόν and πολλῶν is elliptical, implicit in the structure rather than explicit in the meaning:

πολλῶν ἐπέβαν καιρὸν οὐ ψεύδει βαλών

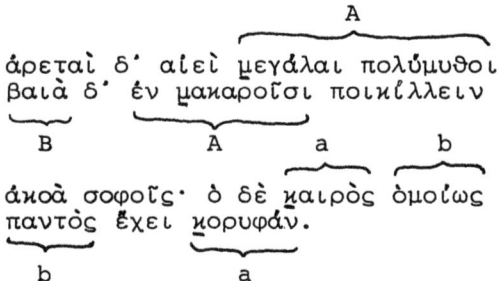

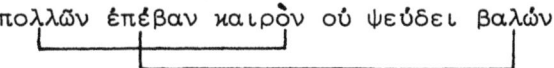

BIBLIOGRAPHY

Allen, W. S. 1973. Accent and rhythm. Prosodic features of Latin and Greek: A study in theory and reconstruction. Cambridge.

Ameis, K. F. 1879. Anhang zu Homers Ilias. Leipzig.

Arnold, E. V. 1905. Vedic metre in its historical development. Cambridge.

Arnold, T. K., ed. 1852. Homer's Iliad. London.

Atkins, S. D. 1968. The RV dyaús-paradigm and the Sievers-Edgerton law. Journal of the American Oriental Society 88.679-709.

Bandu, V. 1963. A grammatical word-index to Ṛgveda. Hoshiarpur.

Bartholomae, C. 1904. Altiranisches Wörterbuch. Strassburg.

Benveniste, E. 1955. Homophonies radicales en indo-européen. Bulletin de la Société de Linguistique de Paris 51.14-41.

________. 1966. Problèmes de linguistique générale. Paris.

________. 1969. Le vocabulaire des institutions indo-européennes. I, II. Paris.

Beye, C. R. 1973. The rhythm of Hesiod's Works and Days. Harvard Studies in Classical Philology 76.23-43.

Bhawe, S. S., ed. 1957. The Soma-hymns of the Rigveda I, II. Baroda.

Björck, G. 1937-1938. πεῖραρ. Mélanges Boisacq 143-148. Brussels.

Boedeker, D. D. 1974. Aphrodite's entry into Greek Epic. Leiden.

Böhtlingk, O. and Roth, R. 1855-1875. Sanskrit-Wörterbuch. St. Petersburg.

Bowra, C. M., trans. 1969. The odes of Pindar. New York.

Brandreth, T. A., ed. 1841. ΩΜΗΡΟΥ ΙΛΙΑΣ. London.

Bundy, E. 1962. Studia Pindarica I, II. Berkeley.

Burn, A. R. 1960. The lyric age of Greece. New York.

Burrow, T. 1955. The sanskrit language. London.

Burton, R. W. B. 1962. Pindar's Pythian odes: Essays in interpretation. Oxford.

Campbell, D. A. 1967. Greek lyric poetry. London.

Carne-Ross, D. S. 1963. Postscript. Patrocleia of Homer 51-62. Trans. C. Logue. Bloomington.

Chantraine, P. 1955. La formation des noms en grec ancien. Paris.

________. 1963. Grammaire homérique I, II. Paris.

Cole, A. T. 1972. Classical Greek and Latin. Versification: Major language types. Sixteen essays 66-68. Ed. W. K. Wimsatt. New York.

Combellack, F. M. 1959. Milman Parry and Homeric artistry. Comparative Literature 11.193-208.

Cookesley, C. G., ed. 1753. Pindari carmina. London.

Clarke, S., ed. 1824. Homeri Ilias. London.

Detienne, M. and Vernant, J.-P. 1974. Les ruses de l'intelligence. La mètis des grecs. Paris.

Dodds, E. R., Palmer, L. R., and Gray, D. H. F. 1968. Homer. Fifty years (and twelve) of Classical scholarship 1-49. London.

Doederlein, D. L., ed. 1863. Homeri Ilias. Leipzig.

Donlan, W. 1971. Homer's Agamemnon. Classical World 65. 109-115.

Dover, K. J. 1964. The poetry of Archilochus. Archiloque 183-222. Fondation Hardt Entretiens 10. Geneva.

Dunbar, H. 1880. A complete concordance to the Odyssey of Homer. Oxford. Revised ed. by B. Marzullo 1962. Hildesheim.

Duntzer, H., ed. 1866. Homers Ilias. Paderborn.

Edwards, G. P. 1971. The language of Hesiod in its traditional context. Oxford.

Edwards, M. 1966. Some features of Homeric craftsmanship. Transactions of the American Philological Association 97.115-179.

________. 1969. On some 'answering' expressions in Homer. Classical Philology 64.81-87.

Ernest, I. A., ed. 1824. Homeri opera omnia. Leipzig.

Faesi, J. V., ed. 1865. Homers Iliade. Berlin.

Farnell, L. R. 1932. The works of Pindar, translated with literary and critical commentaries I-III. London.

Fatouros, G. 1966. Index Verborum zur frühgriechischen Lyrik. Heidelberg.

Fenik, B. 1968. Typical battle scenes in the Iliad. Studies in the narrative techniques of Homeric battle scenes. Wiesbaden.

________. 1974. Studies in the Odyssey. Wiesbaden.

Fennell, C. A. M., ed. 1898. Pindar: The Olympian and Pythian odes. Oxford.

Fitzgerald, R., trans. 1963. Homer, The Odyssey. New York.

________, trans. 1974. Homer, The Iliad. New York.

Fónagy, I. 1963. Die Metaphern in der Phonetik. The Hague.

Frame, D. G. 1971. The origins of Greek ΝΟΥΣ. Dissertation, Harvard University.

Frisk, H. 1960-1970. Griechisches etymologisches Wörterbuch I, II. Heidelberg.

Geldner, K. F. 1951. Der Rig-Veda, aus dem Sanskrit ins Deutsche übersetzt I-IV. Leipzig.

Gildersleeve, B. L., ed. 1890. Pindar, the Olympian and Pythian odes. New York.

Grassmann, H. 1955. Wörterbuch zum Rigveda. Wiesbaden.

Greene, W. C. 1951. The spoken and the written word. Harvard Studies in Classical Philology 55.23-59.

Griffith, J. G. 1968. Early Greek lyric poetry. Fifty years (and twelve) of classical scholarship 50-87. London.

Hainsworth, J. B. 1968. The flexibility of the Homeric formula. Oxford.

________. 1969. Homer. Oxford.

________. 1970. The criticism of an oral Homer. Journal of Hellenic Studies 90.90-98.

Hamm, E.-M. 1958. Grammatik zu Sappho und Alkaios. Berlin.

Harvey, A. E. 1957. Homeric epithets in Greek lyric poetry. Classical Quarterly 7.206-223.

Havelock, E. A. 1963. Preface to Plato. Cambridge, Mass.

Heyne, C. G., ed. 1832. Homerus Ilias. Leipzig.

Hoekstra, A. 1957. Hésiode et la tradition orale. Mnemosyne 10.193-225.

________. 1965. Homeric modifications of formulaic prototypes: Studies in the development of Greek epic diction. Amsterdam.

________. 1969. The sub-epic stage of the formulaic tradition. Studies in the Homeric hymns to Apollo, to Aphrodite and to Demeter. Amsterdam and London.

Holoka, J. P. 1973. Homeric originality: A survey.

Classical World 66.257-293.

Householder, F. W., and Nagy, G. 1972. Greek. Current Trends in Linguistics IX.2, 735-816.

Howald, E. 1946. Der Dichter der Ilias. Zurich.

Ingalls, D. H. H. 1971. Remarks on Mr. Wasson's Soma. Journal of the American Oriental Society 91.188-191.

Ingalls, W. B. 1970. The structure of the Homeric hexameter: A review. Phoenix 24.1-12.

________. 1972. Another dimension of the Homeric formula. Phoenix 26.111-122.

Irigoin, J. 1953. Recherches sur les mètres de la lyrique chorale grecque. Paris.

Jakobson, R. 1960. Linguistics and poetics. Style in language 350-377. Ed. T. Sebeok. Cambridge, Mass.

Kirk, G. S. 1962. The structure and aim of the Theogony. Hésiode et son influence 61-95. Fondation Hardt Entretiens 7. Geneva.

________. 1966. Studies in some technical aspects of Homeric style: I. The structure of the Homeric hexameter; II. Verse-structure and sentence-structure in Homer. Yale Classical Studies 20.72-152.

________, ed. 1967. The language and background of Homer. Cambridge.

Kirkwood, G. M. 1974. Early Greek monody: The history of a poetic type. Ithaca and London.

Krause, W. 1936. Die Ausdrücke für das Schicksal bei Homer. Glotta 25.143-152.

Krischer, T. 1971. Formale Konventionen der homerischen Epik. Munich.

Lanata, G. 1966. Sul linguaggio amoroso di Saffo. Quaderni Urbinati di Cultura Classica 2.63-79.

Latacz, J. 1968. ἄπτερος μῦθος--ἄπτερος φάτις. Glotta 46.27-47.

Lattimore, R., trans. 1947. The odes of Pindar. Chicago.

________, trans. 1951. The Iliad of Homer. Chicago.

Leaf, W., ed. 1971. The Iliad I, II. Amsterdam.

________ and Bayfield, M. A., eds. 1936. The Iliad of Homer I, II. London.

Lefkowitz, M. R. 1963. τῶ καὶ ἐγὼ: The first person in Pindar. Harvard Studies in Classical Philology 67. 177-253.

________. 1973. Critical stereotypes and the poetry of Sappho. Greek, Roman and Byzantine Studies 14. 113-123.

Leumann, M. 1950. Homerische Wörter. Basel.

Longo, O. 1963-1964. Moduli Epici in Saffo, Fr. 1. Atti dell' Insituto Veneto di Scienze, Lettere ed Arti 122. 343-366.

Lord, A. B. 1960. The singer of tales. Cambridge, Mass.

MacDonell, A. A. and Keith, A. B. 1958. Vedic index of names and subjects. London.

Mayrhofer, M. 1956. Kurzgefasstes etymologisches Wörterbuch des Altindischen. Heidelberg.

Meillet, A. 1923. Les origines indo-européennes des mètres grecs. Paris.

________, and Vendryes, J. 1966. Traité de grammaire comparée des langues classiques. Paris.

Merry, W. W. and Riddell, J., eds. 1886. Homer's Odyssey. Oxford.

Muellner, L. 1973. The meaning of Homeric εὔχομαι through its formulas. Dissertation, Harvard University.

Munro, D. B., ed. 1847. Homer, Iliad. Oxford.

Myers, E., ed. 1895. The extant odes of Pindar. London.

Nagler, M. N. 1967. Towards a generative view of the

oral formula. Transactions of the American Philological Association 98.269-311.

________. 1974. Spontaneity and tradition: A study in the oral art of Homer. Berkeley, Los Angeles and London.

Nagy, G. 1970. Greek dialects and the transformation of an Indo-European process. Cambridge, Mass.

________. 1973. Phaethon, Sappho's Phaon, and the white rock of Leukas. Harvard Studies in Classical Philology 77.137-177.

________. 1974. Comparative studies in Greek and Indic meter. Cambridge, Mass.

Niedermann, M. 1931. Zur lateinischen und griechischen Wortgeschichte. Glotta 19.1-15.

Notopoulos, J. A. 1938. Mnemosyne in oral literature. Transactions of the American Philological Association 69.465-493.

________. 1960. Homer, Hesiod and the Achaean heritage of oral poetry. Hesperia 29.177-197.

________. 1964. Studies in early Greek oral poetry. Harvard Studies in Classical Philology 68.1-77.

Olderberg, H. 1909-1912. Ṛgveda, textcritische und exegetische Noten I, II. Berlin.

O'Neill, E. G. 1942. The localization of metrical word-types in the Greek hexameter. Yale Classical Studies 8.102-176.

Onians, R. B. 1951. The origins of European thought. Cambridge.

Page, D. L. 1955. Sappho and Alcaeus: An introduction to the study of ancient Lesbian poetry. Oxford.

________. 1964. Archilochus and the oral tradition. Archiloque 119-179. Fondation Hardt Entretiens 10. Geneva.

Paley, F. A., ed. 1871. The Iliad of Homer. London.

Parry, A. 1956. The language of Achilles. Transactions of the American Philological Association 87.1-7.

________. 1966. Have we Homer's Iliad? Yale Classical Studies 20.177-216.

________, ed. and trans. 1971. The making of Homeric verse: The collected papers of Milman Parry. Oxford.

Parry, A. A. 1973. Blameless Aigisthos: A study of AMYMΩN and other Homeric epithets. Leiden.

Patzer, H. 1972. Dichterische Kunst und poetisches Handwerk im homerischen Epos. Wiesbaden.

Peabody, H. B. 1971. Hesiod, Works and Days: An exemplar of ancient Greek oral composition. Albany.

Peradotto, J. 1974. Odyssey 8.564-571: Verisimilitude, narrative analysis, and bricolage. Texas Studies in Literature and Language 15.803-832.

Pischell, R. and Geldner, K. F. 1889-1901. Vedische Studien. Stuttgart.

Pokorny, J. 1954. Indogermanisches etymologisches Wörterbuch. Bern.

Pope, M. W. M. 1960. Athena's development in Homeric epic. American Journal of Philology 81.113-135.

________. 1963. The Parry-Lord theory of Homeric composition. Acta Classica 6.1-21.

Porter, H. N. 1951. The early Greek hexameter. Yale Classical Studies 12.3-63.

Prendergast, G. L. 1875. A complete concordance to the Iliad of Homer. London. Revised ed. by B. Marzullo 1962. Hildesheim.

Privitera, G. A. 1967. La rete de Afrodite. Ricerche sulla prima ode di Saffo. Quaderni Urbinati di Cultura Classica 4.7-58.

Renou, L. 1955-1969. Etudes védiques et pāṇinéennes I-XVII. Paris.

Ṛgveda-Samhitā with the Commentary of Sāyaṇāchārya. 1933-

1951. Poona.

Rosenmeyer, T. G. 1965. The formula in early Greek poetry. Arion 4.295-311.

Ruck, C. A. P. and Matheson, W. H.- trans. 1968. Pindar: Selected odes, translated with interpretive essays. Ann Arbor.

Ruijgh, C. J. 1968. A propos d'une nouvelle application de méthodes structuralistes à la langue Homérique. Mnemosyne 21.113-131.

Russo, J. A. 1966. The structural formula in Homeric verse. Yale Classical Studies 20.217-240.

________. 1968. Homer against his tradition. Arion 7.275-295.

________. 1974. The inner man in Archilochus and the Odyssey. Greek, Roman and Byzantine Studies 15.139-152.

Schmitt, R. 1967. Dichtung und dichtersprache in indogermanischen Zeit. Wiesbaden.

Schultze, W. 1933. Kleine schriften. Göttingen.

Schulze, W. S. 1892. Quaestiones epicae. Gutersloh.

Segal, C. P. 1971a. Andromache's anagnorisis: Formulaic artistry in Iliad 22.437-476. Harvard Studies in Classical Philology 75.33-57.

________. 1971b. The theme of the mutilation of the corpse in the Iliad. Leiden.

Shannon, R. S. 1975. The arms of Achilles and Homeric compositional technique. Leiden.

Snell, B. 1962. Griechische Metrik. Göttingen.

Stanford, W. B. 1936. Greek Metaphor. Oxford.

________, ed. 1959. The Odyssey of Homer I, II. London.

________. 1969. Euphonic reasons for the choice of Homeric formulae. Hermathena 108.14-17.

Thieme, P. 1957. Review of Renou 1955-1969. Journal of the American Oriental Society 77.51-56.

Treu, M. 1955. Von Homer zur Lyrik. Munich.

Trollope, W., ed. 1827. Iliad of Homer. London.

van Groningen, B. A. 1958. La composition littéraire archaïque grecque: Procédés et réalizations. Amsterdam.

________, ed. 1966. Theognis, le premier livre. Amsterdam.

Van Leeuwen, J., ed. 1913. Ilias. Leiden.

Van Sickle, J. 1975. The new erotic fragment of Archilochus. Quaderni Urbinati di Cultura Classica 20. Forthcoming.

Velenkar, H. D. 1963. Ṛgveda Mandala VII. Bombay.

Wackernagel, J. 1905. Altindische Grammatik. Göttingen.

Wasson, R. G. 1968. Soma: Divine mushroom of immortality. New York.

West, M. L. 1966. Hesiod Theogony. Oxford.

________. 1973a. Indo-European metre. Glotta 51.161-187.

________. 1973b. Greek poetry 2000-700 B.C. The Classical Quarterly 22.179-192.

________. 1974. Studies in Greek elegy and iambus. Berlin and New York.

Whallon, W. 1969. Formula, character and context: Studies in Homeric, Old English, and Old Testament poetry. Washington, D.C. and Cambridge, Mass.

Whitman, C. H. 1958. Homer and the heroic tradition. Cambridge, Mass.

________. 1974. Foreward. Comparative studies in Greek and Indic meter vii-xiii. Nagy 1974. Cambridge, Mass.

Whitney, W. D. 1873. Oriental and linguistic studies: The Veda; the Avesta; the science of language. New York.

Witte, K. 1913. Homeros: Sprache. Real-Encyclopädie der klassischen Altertumswissenschaft VIII 2213-2247.

Young, David C. 1968. Three odes of Pindar. Leiden.

________. 1970. Pindaric criticism. Pindaros und Bacchylides 1-95. Eds. W. M. Calder and J. Stearn. Wege und Forschung 134. Darmstadt.

________. 1971. Pindar Isthmian 7, myth and exempla. Leiden.

Young, Douglas, ed. 1961. Theognis. Leipzig.

INDEX LOCORUM

Aelian
29 Hercher: 186C

Alkaios
Z21: 124-132, 166-167
Z27: 122-124, 130-132, 168

Apollonius Rhodius
A.R. 4.1201-1202: 187D

Archilochos
106.5: 117n
111: 115-119, 136, 168, 176
112.2: 117n
119.1: 117
122.5: 117
122.8: 117
124(b).3: 117n
128.6: 117n
130.1: 117n
132: 117n
133.3: 117
134: 117n
219-221: 116-117

Aristophanes
Ra. 1463-1464: 37n

Aristotle
H.A. 501a18: 49
Po. 21.11-13: 34n

Euripides
Heracl. 836: 49

Herakleitos
62: 58n

Herodotus
I.74.4: 50

Hesiod
Theogony
333-335: 107-108, 110-112

Hesiod
Theogony
517-532: 28n, 107-108, 112-113
622: 106-107, 113-114
637-638: 55-56
720: 115
728: 115
731: 114
736-741: 114-115
738=809: 106-107
809=738: 106-107
Works and Days
166-174: 27n, 106-107, 109-110
518: 107

Homer
Iliad
I 98: 127
157: 118
254=VII 124: 61
384: 192J
386: 192J
II 15: 187-188E
111=IX 18: 40n
144: 118
155: 128
171: 60
324: 190H
489-493: 142
III 116: 191J
260: 192J
408: 60
IV 416: 128
V 3: 12
20: 191J
VI 6: 53n
143: 35-37, 164, 175
285: 60n
528: 192J
VII 6: 191J
101-102: 34-35, 116-118, 136,

Homer
Iliad
VII
101-102: 164, 176, 187D
124=I 254: 61
402: 38-40, 174, 188E
416: 191J
478-479: 34

VIII 478: 11
478-481: 25, 27n, 34-35
IX 18=II 111: 40n
413: 127
XI 106: 52
117: 60
336: 55
608: 51
XII 79: 38-40, 174, 187E
417-425: 53n
432-436: 56
XIII 37: 52
345-357: 171-172
358-360: 10-11, 22, 39n, 45-57, 64, 165, 170-173, 189G, 190-191I.
798: 118
XIV 200-201=301-302: 24, 29
301-302=200-201: 24, 29
389-391: 54-55
XV 208=XVI 52: 60
410-413: 56-57
XVI 52=XV 208: 60
475: 190H
XVII 318: 43n
XVIII 2: 127
242: 51
501: 43-45, 178, 186D
XIX 113: 61
307: 60
XX 48: 51
100-101: 55
429: 35-37, 164, 175
XXI 66: 61
XXIII 258: 43n
350: 20, 41-43, 178, 187D, 190H
375: 190H
486-487: 44

Homer
Iliad
XXIII
741: 191J
758: 190H
761: 151, 177
XXIV 278: 192J
Odyssey
i 14: 43n
324: 192J
ii 29: 128
41: 60
434: 100
iii 103: 60n
433: 31-34, 164, 178, 186C
iv 35: 60n
83: 191J
130: 192J
298: 191J
455: 33
511: 127
529: 32
563-564: 25-26, 27n, 107, 110n
812: 60n
v 288-290: 22, 28n, 57-61, 108, 165, 176
289: 11
414: 61
457: 60
vi 111: 128
144: 128
169: 60
vii 265: 128
324: 192J
viii 62=471: 191J
121: 190H
159: 192J
275: 52
327: 32-33
332: 32-33
471=62: 191J
ix 29: 43n
283-285: 23-24, 27-29, 163-164
x 353: 191J
xi 13-14: 25
121-136: 30n

Homer
Odyssey
xi
620-622: 59n
xii 37: 188F
43: 39
50-51: 37-40, 64, 164, 186C
160-162: 37-40, 164
179=162=51: 37-40, 164
191: 39
xiv 283: 43n
xvii 519: 192J
xviii 81: 60
212: 51
217: 61
274: 60
323: 128
495: 192J
xix 100: 192J
105: 192J
532: 61
xx 277: 192J
xxii 33: 38-40, 174, 187E
41: 38-40, 174, 187E
175=192: 188F
xxiii 248-249: 28-31, 59n, 123, 129, 136, 145, 164, 175-176
xxiv 160: 128

Homeric Hymns
h. Ap. 129: 11, 20, 39n, 40-43, 64, 113n
228: 191J
h. Merc. 47-48: 188F
317-318: 32
h. Ven. 227: 24, 29

Isocrates
Panegyricus 5: 186C

Pigres: 133-136, 142

Pindar
*O.*2.31: 36n, 146-147, 169
2.68-77: 27n

Pindar
O.
13.44-48: 155n
*P.*1: 155-162
1.81-83: 148-162, 169, 177
4.220: 144-146, 168-169, 178
4.285-286: 155n
8.29-32: 154
9.76f.: 154n, 193L
*N.*1.18: 193L
7.19: 36n
10.19-20: 154
Paean 9.49: 190H

Plutarch
Luc. 21.5: 49

Posidippus
26.17 Kock: 186C

Rigveda
1.9.1: 79-80
1.61.12: 68-69, 183
1.94.4: 78-79, 183
1.97.8: 97
1.140.12: 97
1.162.18: 84-85, 184
1.174.9: 98
2.15.5: 98
2.33.3: 98
4.19.3: 70
4.19.9: 70-71, 183
4.22.2: 80-82, 88-91, 182
4.30.17: 98
6.4.8: 99
7.50.2: 83-84, 182
7.60.12: 99
7.70.2: 99
7.103.5: 74-77, 183
8.16.11: 97
8.48.5: 73-74, 182
9.15.6: 87-88, 180
9.73.1: 97
10.53.1: 85-86, 181
10.68.9: 66-67, 180
10.79.7: 71, 181
10.87.5: 68, 182

Rigveda
10.89.8: 69, 183
10.97.12: 83, 184
10.100.5: 86-87, 181
10.163.6: 72-73, 184

Sappho
1: 103n
31: 103n
44: 16, 120, 124-129, 166, 191-192J
168: 19

Solon
4.14f.: 137n
16: 132-139, 158n, 168

Theognis
19-30: 102n
78: 143
139-140: 133-136, 140-141, 143
180: 143
182=684=752: 143
324: 143
392: 143
588: 143
638: 143
646: 143
684=182=752: 143
752=182=684: 143
1077-1078: 133-136, 140-141
1172-1173: 133-136, 139-140
1308: 143

Xenophon
Cyn. 5.20: 49

Vergil
Aen. 1.342: 149

www.ingramcontent.com/pod-product-compliance
Ingram Content Group UK Ltd.
Pitfield, Milton Keynes, MK11 3LW, UK
UKHW041430180426
11947UKWH00007B/366

9 780891 302421